THEY DREW FIRE

THEY DREW FIRE

Combat Artists of World War II

Brian Lanker

Nicole Newnham

TV Books

New York

Library of Congress Cataloging-in-Publication Data

    Lanker, Brian.
       They drew fire : combat artists of World War II / by Brian Lanker and Nicole
     Newnham.
    p. cm.
    Contents: Ed Reep—Manuel Bromberg—Richard Gibney—William Draper—
Robert Greenhalgh—Howard Brodie—Franklin Boggs.
    ISBN: 1-57500-085-7
    1. World War, 1939-1945—Art and the war. 2. Artists—United States—History—20th century. I. Newnham, Nicole. II. Title.
    D810.L36 2000
    704.94994054—dc21
                                              99-086620

Current photos of artists by Brian Lanker.

The publisher has made every effort to secure permission to reproduce copyrighted material and would like to apologize should there have been any errors or omissions.

TV Books, L.L.C.
1619 Broadway, Ninth Floor
New York, NY 10019
www.tvbooks.com

Interior design by Tania Garcia
Manufactured in the United States of America

Contents

Introduction

Brian Lanker

My wife, Lynda, is an artist, many of my friends are artists, and when I was younger I spent time taking private painting lessons.

Creating fine art under the best of circumstances, the calmest of studio conditions, with the most controllable atmosphere, is in itself a very difficult and painstaking accomplishment. So when my friend John Frook told me that artists with paintbrushes and rifles were working from foxholes and tents in the middle of battle during World War II, I was stopped in my tracks. How many of them were there? How did they do this? How many pieces of their artwork have survived? And most of all, why?

John happened to read a short article that mentioned Howard Brodie, a soldier artist in World War II. The intriguing revelation that someone in the Army had the assignment to create art out of the chaos of war was not lost on John. We immediately launched an exhaustive search to determine if there were others. Were they alive? What happened to their artwork? And what did it reveal to us about the war?

When I would speak to others and mention this story, they almost always responded the same way: "You're kidding! I've never heard of this before. Tell me more." Certainly this was an untold story. Quite simply, at that time a documentary film was born, and it was one that would need to be moved on quickly if we were going to be able to record the artists' stories firsthand. Preliminary research revealed that more than one hundred combat artists participated in World War II, and most of them were deceased. No single event in the history of mankind was more documented in art while it happened than World War II, and now most of the voices of these special artists were forever silent. This added an urgency and dedication to our project.

Before long a few names and phone numbers emerged.

"Hello, is this Ed Reep?"

"Yes."

"Captain Ed Reep?"

"Yes."

"The Captain Ed Reep who was a combat artist in World War II?"

"Yes."

"Well, thank God you're alive."

Soon we had gotten a number of similar responses on the other end of the phone. And they were interested in telling their stories. We found that the joy of hearing their voices was matched by the excitement of seeing for the first time the art these World War II artists had created.

More than twelve thousand paintings and drawings were created by the U.S. combat artists of World War II, and when the war ended their work

Opposite: Hurd, Detail of *Lt. Thomas Borders*

was stuck away in military archives, preserved but seldom, if ever, seen by the general public.

Over two thousand works of art painted by Army artists in World War II were in the basement of an office building in downtown Washington, D.C., curated by the U.S. Center for Military History. They were hung on sliding metal racks and lay in flat files in a temperature-controlled basement, along with drawings and paintings from the Revolutionary War, the Civil War, Korea, and Vietnam. We would often gasp, as we slid open a rack or turned a corner: one might find a shocking Picasso-like abstraction of corpses in India, a child receiving a lollipop from a soldier in war-torn France, or night bombing in Berlin as seen from the cockpit of a plane in startling color. It was as if the war, which we knew mostly from black-and-white newsreels and Hollywood movies, was becoming a color-saturated, detailed reality, in all of its horror and mundanity. Trips to the Navy and Marine archives revealed similar treasures.

We visited Peter Harrington (at Brown University), who has been passionately collecting and archiving World War II combat art for the past ten years. Through advertisements in veterans' magazines and other outlets, he met many artists — both official and amateur — or their families. They had notebooks filled with sketches of their lives as soldiers and completed paintings perhaps considered too shocking by the military, or even themselves, at the time. In some cases they had entire collections. Most of these items had been sitting in attics, in closets, in basements, unseen since the war. Now, added to the Brown collection, they are an incredibly valuable pictorial resource for the future generations who will study World War II.

Harrington is a military historian, and he encouraged us to look at the World War II combat art with the proper historical perspective. As different as the World War II combat art is from other depictions of battle, it stands firmly rooted in a long tradition of military iconography. As we read old letters and journals and opened dusty out-of-print books from military booksellers, it became clear that both the military and the artists of World War II understood this.

"Art and War," wrote Brigadier General Denig, the founder of the Marine Corps art program, "are old companions. Battlefields and soldiers have been popular subjects with artists since earliest times. The deeds of armies and the glories of great warriors were chronicled in statuary, poetry, song, and picture long before Greece brought about what is considered modern civilization."

Indeed, from the Grecian urn to the Roman tomb or monument, war — such a fundamental part of the human existence — has also been one of man's great artistic themes. *The Bayeux Tapestry*, which depicts William the Conqueror's invasion of England, was woven together from soldiers' battlefield stories by the ladies of William's court. While artistic depictions of military events in the medieval period were purely representational, during the Renaissance artists — including Leonardo da Vinci and Michelangelo — were commissioned by the nobility to paint tableaux that glorified the victors, often focusing on individual heroes. This trend continued in modern history, notably in the work of Delacroix and Gericault in France and Benjamin West in Canada.

The horrors of man's violence against man have also been tackled by artists throughout history. Any modern artist who takes brush or pen to the topic of war cannot help but have been influenced by Goya's satiric and graphic depictions of atrocities committed by the Spanish army during the Peninsula War.

America's first "combat artist," it could be argued, was John Trumbull, the "painter of the American Revolution." He left art school to enlist in the Continental Army as a private. He marched to Boston with the First Connecticut regiment, and was witness to the Battle of Bunker Hill. Responding to General Washington's request for a drawing of the enemy position, he snuck out in the dark to view the number and placement of the enemy's mounted guns. His drawing was delivered to Washington and he was shortly thereafter appointed second aide de camp. He went on to paint large battle scenes, inspired by on-the-spot sketches.

With the increasing affordability of lithography and printing, art could be reproduced in large numbers in weekly magazines and newspapers, and this became the primary way for Americans to get visual information about current events. Winslow Homer, widely regarded as the greatest of all nineteenth century painters, went to the front during the Civil War as a correspondent-illustrator for the magazine *Harper's Weekly*. He covered the Peninsular Campaign from Yorktown to the Battle of Mulavern Hill. His war art, like much of his work, focused on the human element: soldiers on furlough, playing cards, receiving Christmas packages. The World War II artists who would later draw and paint for *Life* and *Yank* magazines were very aware that they followed in his footsteps. Robert Greenhalgh, who began his career as a magazine illustrator just before Pearl Harbor, remembered seeing Homer's "wonderful paintings" as a youngster and thinking, "Gee, that would be good, to be a war artist. But of course, I had no idea that such a thing might ever come to pass."

During World War I the War Department decided to send artists into the field to make a pictorial record of the war. Eight artists selected by Charles Dana Gibson were sent to France to record the activities of the American Expeditionary Forces. Much of the resulting work was more honest and brutal than had probably been foreseen. The renowned artist and illustrator Kerr Eby published a collection of his World War I art; entitled simply *War*, it remains one of the most powerful anti-war statements ever published. This artwork influenced the combat artists of World War II, as did the expressionistic and cubist art that flowed from the brushes of many modern artists in response to the fresh memory of the horrors of modern warfare. Ernst Ludwig Kirchner and Max Beckmann returned from the trenches of World War I to paint powerful expressionistic paintings of the human cost of war in Germany. Paul Nash, Christopher Nevinson, and Wyndham Lewis are among the British artists who were sent to experience combat firsthand and then paint their impressions for posterity. And of course, arguably the pinnacle of modern anti-war paintings, Picasso's *Guernica* conveys with raw emotion and pain the devastation caused by the aerial bombardment of Guernica during the Spanish Civil War. There can be no doubt that World War II artists perceived themselves as part of this great tradition as they marched into battle.

And yet, World War II was different. It seemed incongruous to us that the most massive effort to involve artists in documenting battle occurred during the same war that is famous for being so well captured in newsreels and photographs. What was the artist expected to capture that the camera could not? Frederick Voss, a curator and historian at the National Portrait Gallery, explained to us that at the time—and I suppose it is still true—to *paint* something gave it a sense of importance or permanence.

Additionally, from the military perspective, artists could paint things that the camera, at that point, was incapable of recording—night scenes, for instance. Or color. Color photography was still in its infancy on the eve of World War II. And an artist could paint his impression of an important scene while at the same time taking care to omit details that might compromise national security if released to the general public.

(We were surprised, in fact, that the few references to censorship we found in the archives of the various collections were in regard to this kind of technical detail: please omit the name and number of this plane, or please correct this mechanical detail.) The United States was not alone in sending artists into battle: almost every country that fought during World War II had its own combat art program.

A very large percentage of the World War II drawings could not be considered propaganda by any stretch of the imagination. Rather, they aimed to tell an honest and often brutal truth about the nature of war. And what amazed us was that it was *this* endeavor that was specifically encouraged and supported by the armed services, national publications, and private companies who funded the artists. We also found it surprising that the artists were specifically encouraged to paint or draw in whatever style they chose—expressionism, realism, whatever allowed the artists to best express the truth of their experiences.

In the basement archives of Abbott Laboratories, who funded an extensive combat art program during World War II, we found evidence of the importance of the artwork to people at the time. Photographs of combat artists at work in the field frequently showed eager crowds of soldiers standing around them, watching their sketches or drawings come to life. The artists commented in letters and journals about the profound impact that seeing themselves rendered in pencil, ink, and paint had on the soldiers. They gave their addresses to the artists by the hundreds, asking for copies of their portrait, or a drawing of the battle they had just fought in, the ship they lived on. When a painting of any regiment, ship, or battle appeared in a national magazine, it would be followed up by requests from parents: "My *son fought in that battle. We don't know of his whereabouts . . . would it be possible to have a copy of the drawing?*" A doctor who had

used reproductions of some of the combat art to decorate a hospital in Manila wrote to Abbott Laboratories expressing his thanks for the "intangible physical, mental, and morale contributions that your collections have made towards our therapies." In many cases the portraits made by combat artists of fighter pilots, medics, and infantrymen would be the last images of them ever recorded. Everyone involved seemed to realize the importance of entering these faces and actions into our collective visual history.

But this forgotten chapter of American history most came to life for us as producers Nicole Newnham, Bonni Cohen, and myself began to venture into the seaside towns, woodsy artist colonies, and sunlit studios that the artists have chosen to call home since the war. (All of the artists in our film, and others with whom we consulted, went on to lead successful artistic lives after the war, and all of them felt that it was their experience as combat artists that had jumpstarted their careers.) The graciousness and warmth with which we were welcomed impressed and delighted us. One of the more pleasant afternoons I've spent in my life was at the home of Manuel Bromberg and his wife Jane in Woodstock. Bromberg, in the process of creating a beautiful and massive sculpture from a cliffside cast in fiberglass, served us cheese and wine and told us stories about meeting Picasso and Bonnard in Paris during the war.

More than one artist was surprised at our intense interest in his career as a combat artist, a part of history that they had assumed would remain forgotten. But our discussions almost always unleashed an outpouring of memories and impressions of war, rendered more vivid in their memories than most veterans' by the artistic process they had gone through at the time. If we asked for the story behind a particular painting, the artist began to remember the colors, sounds, tastes of their experience—all of the different elements they had attempted to express through their painting.

I remember Ed Reep's face lighting up as he opened his old World War II trunk for us, his hands moving tenderly across the "artist correspondent" patch that had been hand embroidered for him by Italian partisan women and unfolding the map of Europe he had carried with him throughout the war, carefully coloring in red crayon each new Allied advance. Often, we were shown paintings that had been rejected by the government for archiving after the war, or the little sketchbooks the artists had carried with them. Some of these pieces were among the most moving and interesting we saw.

We were lucky enough to see the combat artist in action when we followed Howard Brodie to the Mojave Desert, where he was working on drawings of the modern American soldier commissioned by General Sullivan of the USO. Tall, handsome, and incredibly sensitive and intelligent, Howard, now eighty-five, worked tirelessly to really understand and relate to his subjects, accompanying them on a mock-battle in the cold and windy desert surrounding Fort Irwin. Even as he applied himself to learning about the overwhelming amount of new technology that surrounds the modern soldier, Howard—today as in World War II—unfailingly sees the human side of the military. That is what makes his art so brilliant.

For thirty-four years I have been a photojournalist for newspapers and magazines. I was a contract photographer for *Life* magazine and *Sports Illustrated*. Photography has been a large part of my life, so it is not unusual that I would feel close to the iconographic images of World War II: Joe Rosenthal's memorable image of the flag raising on Mt. Suribachi, Iwo Jima; Robert Capa's gripping photos from the Normandy invasion; and many more. My visual understanding of the war was molded by photography. But now I have a new and different understanding of World War II. A vibrant rich, emotional picture has emerged.

Since the war we have lost contact with these wonderful works of art and we have known little or nothing at all of those who risked their lives to create this legacy—until now.

The Army Art Program

Some of the men are looking at my drawings. It does not occur to them that there can be technically good or bad drawings . . . *the drawings are them.* Each drawing has the name and rank of the sitter, the date, and place. The men continually ask: "What will happen to these drawings, Mr. Biddle? Suppose after the war I want to see one and show it to my wife? Could I get a copy?" The likeness is not flattering, perhaps not recognizable. It is *him,* though, and he is going down in history. *Him,* an atom of the great, anonymous, American people's Army."

—George Biddle, U.S. Army Artist

The bombing of Pearl Harbor shocked the United States out of a comfortable isolationism. Artists, like most Americans, eagerly sought ways to contribute their skills to the war effort. Some of the country's best young artists had already been drafted into the Army; others were mobilized to enlist. Small soldier art programs flourished in boot camps around the country. Inspired by the success of a small team of civilian artists sent to observe and paint in World War I, the Army began to envision the potential of sending multiple artists into active theaters of war to record and interpret their experiences in what promised to be the most significant of all wars.

In September 1942, Frances Brennan, newly appointed director of the Office of War Information's graphics bureau, was a passionate advocate for the role of the artist in war. In the magazine *Art Bulletin* he wrote:

Certainly now, in the greatest of all wars, is the time to find out if another Goya is still farming in Iowa, or another Daumier

sketches acidly in Vermont. The American People need their artists now—to charge them with the grave responsibility of spelling out their anger, their grief, their greatness, and their justice. The artist will respond, as he has countless times before in the history of the world, to fight it out on the field where no others can.

The essence of art is freedom. Without it, the world of art could not exist. We know that the enemy is trying to destroy freedom—that he has long since chained together his men of talent. We know the total pattern of his wretchedness—we saw it first when he destroyed the works and lives of those whose art was a threat to his evil purposes. And we saw more than the impending war in the light of his fires—we saw ritualism, barbarism, standardization without philosophy, and the inevitable end of truth as decent men had known it. We saw, in short, an unprincipled plan to degenerate and possess men's minds.

Opposite: Reep, Detail of *We Move Again.* Full image in The Face of War

What this means to art has been said by greater pens than this, but if it needs saying again, it means, quite simply, that if this war is lost, no artist worthy of the name will ever paint again in pursuit of his own imagination.

George Biddle agreed. A mural artist and the brother of the U.S. Secretary General, Biddle went to the assistant secretary of war with the idea of forming an Army war artist unit in January 1943. The unit would send artists to combat areas to paint their impressions of battle. The Corps of Engineers had in fact been developing such a program since early 1942, and Biddle was invited to form a War Department Art Advisory Committee and serve as chair.

Biddle recruited a select group of well-known people from the art world to serve on the advisory committee, which would be responsible for selecting artists. They included the noted artist Henry Varnum Poor, director of the Metropolitan Museum of Art Francis Henry Taylor, director of the National Gallery David Finley, and John Steinbeck. Steinbeck was an active supporter of the war art program and wrote to Biddle:

> It seems to me that a total war would require the use not only of all of the material resources of the nation but also the spiritual and psychological participation of the whole people. And the only psychic communication that we have is through the arts.

Steinbeck hoped to expand the idea to include a body of writers who would accompany the war artists to the various fronts, but the idea never got off the ground.

The committee sent out an introductory letter

Opposite: Biddle, *Death at Troli*

to the selected artists in February. Half of them were military—from the ranks—and half were civilian. Some of the most talented painters of the 1930s and 1940s were among those chosen—the works of Reginald Marsh, Jack Levine, Mitchell Saporin, and Joe Jones are now much desired by major American museums. The letter reached the artists in barracks, studios, and homes around the country, and its introduction must have made their heads spin:

> . . . You have been recommended by the War Department Art Advisory Board as one of a small group of outstanding American artists to go to an active war theater, and there to obtain a graphic record of war. The theaters of war to which you will eventually be assigned include:

1. The Caribbean and South America
2. Southwest Africa (Dakar and Akkra)
3. England and Iceland
4. Northeast Africa and the Near East
5. India, Burma, and China

Although the letter suggested that the artists would have a fair amount of influence over their eventual destination, the chaos of war seems to have intervened. Most artists did not end up in their theater of choice.

A more detailed memorandum, sent by Biddle to the artists in March, outlined the lofty goals and passionate sense of purpose behind the program. It also revealed the surprising amount of freedom and latitude given to the artists, the emphasis on personal expression that distinguished this art program from any previous endeavor.

Above: Baer, *Chinese Stretcher*
Opposite: Gold, *T/5 Duff, Tank Driver*

T/5 Duff
"Tank Driver"

T/Sgt. Albert Gold ETO '44

... Any subject is in order, if as artists you feel that it is part of War; battle scenes and the front line; battle landscapes; the dying and the dead; prisoners of war; field hospitals and base hospitals; wrecked habitations and bombing scenes; character sketches of our own troops, of prisoners, of the natives of the countries you visit;—never official portraits; the tactical implements of war; embarkation and debarkation scenes; the nobility, courage, cowardice, cruelty, boredom of war; all this should form part of a well-rounded picture. Try to omit nothing; duplicate to your heart's content. Express if you can, realistically or symbolically the essence and spirit of war. You may be guided by Blake's mysticism, by Goya's cynicism and savagery, by Delacroix's romanticism, by Daumier's humanity and tenderness; or

better still follow your own inevitable star. We believe that our Army Command is giving you an opportunity to bring back a record of great value to our country. Our Committee wants to assist you to that end.

The memorandum went on to suggest that the artists divide their work into two phases: the sketching and visual note-taking they would do during visits to the front lines, and the "working up" of this material into drawings and paintings that would be sent home for posterity. The latter phase, Biddle noted, would be best accomplished in the rear, where the artists would be given studios. This rough game plan was in fact how most combat artists approached their assignments overseas.

A total of forty-two Army artists were eventually selected by the committee to work in twelve theaters of war around the world. Biddle himself

Above: Bromberg, "Over the Side"
Opposite: Von Ripper, *Dawn Patrol Looks for Enemy*

vas." Still, when the $71,898,425,740 war bill was passed in June, the art program was cut. Funds for the artists would cease on August 31.

The artists were devastated. One artist wrote in his diary, "One of us might conceivably have had his head shot off, and at the same time Congress is giving us this kick in the pants. They might have waited to judge the results of the venture before they moved to wipe out the thing."

Despite the cancellation of the program, most of the artists remained determined to continue their work. *Life* magazine initiated its own war art program, and picked up the contracts of many of the civilian artists. Many of the Army artists were reassigned to information offices overseas where they continued to draw and paint. Some military leaders took advantage of the stranded artists and appointed them "official combat artists" of individual campaigns and units.

In 1944 Congress changed its position and authorized soldier artists to produce artwork outside the U.S. as long as it did not interfere with their regular assignments. Army-supported artists continued to cover the fronts in North Africa, Sicily, Italy, Northern Europe, the South Pacific, Japan, and Korea. Unofficially, soldiers sketched, drew, or painted their wartime impressions and submitted them to the war department.

was appointed the head of the North African unit, headquartered in Algiers. By early May 1943, artists in the South Pacific, Australia, Alaska, and North Africa were hard at work, and the other units were either on standby overseas or awaiting departure clearance.

Unbeknownst to them, the Army art program was under fire at home. In June, the House of Representatives began to examine the Army's budget for the year 1943–44. Of the $71.5 *billion* budget, only $125,000 was slated for the art program. Nevertheless, the necessity of the art program was called into question and most forcefully opposed by Democratic Congressman Joe Starnes of Alabama, who called the project "[a] piece of foolishness." Representative A. Willis Robertson of Virginia defended the program, arguing, "we can take photographs of what happens in Europe, but . . . it takes the vision and artistic skill of the artist to bring us the inspiration which only an artist can put down on can-

The artists were required to send all of their completed paintings and drawings to Washington. By the end of the war the Army had acquired more than two thousand works of art. In June 1945 they established a Historical Properties Section to maintain this collection. The works were viewed by a selection committee and those that were not deemed of sufficient historic value were returned to the artists.

Today, the collection is stored away in the archives of the U.S. Army Center for Military History in downtown Washington, D.C., where it remains a compelling and enduring record of war.

All through the war, I fought the war more furiously perhaps with my paintbrush

than with my weapons. And I always put myself in a position where I could witness

or be a part of the fighting. That was my job, I felt. And I was young, kind of crazy,

I suppose.

Ed Reep

—U. S. Army

I was a buck private.

Did my training in Camp Roberts, California, which was a dust bowl. I was always the shortest guy in the platoon, so I was at the end and I always ate all the dust. The only time I was free was when they said, "To the rear, march." And then I was leading the platoon.

I went to the USO dances. I thought I was Fred Astaire, and my wife, my future wife, tagged me over and over and over again, and I fell in love with her and we married and are married to this day.

I received a telegram when I was on the firing line in Indio, California. A fellow came running up to me and said, "Are you Lieutenant Reep?" and I said, "Yes." He said, "I have a wire for you." And I read the wire, it was from the Secretary of War, Henry Stimson…saying that the War Department Art Advisory Committee is considering you for an artist overseas assignment.

Well, of course I went absolutely bonkers, and almost tripped over the guy next to me who was firing [on the practice line] and right in the line of [his] fire.

And my career began as a war artist.

There were twenty-three soldiers and I believe seventeen, or was it nineteen, civilians selected for this job, War Artists Overseas Corps, and we were all assigned to different theaters of operation. I was assigned to Africa. And of course what we were to do, essentially, was to document the war.

George Biddle was put in charge of indoctrinating all of the units. We received a letter from George and I'm afraid this memorandum, so to speak, was the thing that just about killed us in the eyes of the congressmen, because George Biddle said we could do anything. If you know the Army as I grew to know them, it would be better not to say those things.

The group of war artists were sent a memorandum stating that, "We believe that our Army command is giving you an opportunity to bring back a record of great value to our country. Express if you can, realistically or symbolically, the essence and spirit of war. You may be guided by Blake's mysticism, by Daumier's humanity and tenderness. Or better still, follow your own inevitable star."

Congress said, "This is boondoggling, this is a waste of money and a waste of time." And they cut $125,000 out of a $70 billion budget.

When I found out that the appropriation had been taken away and I was no longer a war artist I was decimated. Totally crushed. It was a dream of mine to fulfill this thing after being selected and being so happy, overjoyed, and almost manic about the whole thing. A war artist, imagine.

Later, George Marshall and Eisenhower reversed that procedure. I have a letter from

Marshall to Eisenhower telling Ike to "Get these artists back to work." I can tell you there are a hell of a lot of high-powered generals and colonels who want everything they do documented.

I received a memo and it said, "Please report to General Eisenhower's office at 0800 hours" or whatever, you see. Everything is very formal and you do it, and I did it. And I was petrified. What in the world would General Eisenhower want with me? Well, when I got there I was ushered into this office and there was the great man. And he said to me, "Lieutenant Reep," and I said, "Yes, sir," and he said, "We have five divisions going into Italy." He said, "There they are on the table." He said, "I want you to pick one division and assign these other four artists to a division. You are going to be painting." And I had to decide very quickly, and one was an armored division so I took it because I hated to walk. And I looked up to tell the General that I had done this and he was gone. He was out in the hall doing

Above: Ed Reep
Right: Tanks Ready to Roll

10

calisthenics and a colonel said, "All right, that'll be fine." And I was dismissed.

I tell you it was all so frightening. It was all so wonderful, I couldn't believe it. It was a fairy tale.

The mandate I felt as a war artist was to paint the war. And scared as I was most of the time, I went to the front almost the first day I got ahold of a vehicle. I drove like mad to the front.

It was my modus operandi — to just paint on location and respond to the thing right then and there. I drew and I was shaking, I was excited.

I was bombed, I was strafed, I was shelled, I was mortared, and there's nothing, nothing worse than being strafed. You think every bullet coming out of the airplane's guns is going for your forehead.

I was painting in the field in Anzio one day, and all of a sudden the Germans decided that the U.S. Army could do with one less artist, and they shelled the devil out of me. And I ran — I ran so fast that I left my helmet and my helmet liner and everything else I had and got into a gully, and then when I came back, I just continued to paint.

I can't say that I was so brave or fearless, but it didn't bother me, I painted up there because, by God, that was my job and I did it. If they shot at me, well, if they missed me I'd run, and they missed me. They missed me every time.

I wanted to stay at the front. So they found a vacated foxhole, never did find out what happened to the guy that had it.

It was a hot night, so I had stripped down and was nude and started to write a letter, and I

Above: Orderly Room at Anzio
Opposite: W.W. Emory Theatre

wrote funny letters, I thought, almost puerile, in a way. But I said, "Dear Family, We had open house last night for lizards, ants, mice, and mosquitoes. Everyone stayed right on including the flies who just dropped in," and I said, "on the fly," which I thought was terribly humorous. And then I wrote, "I can't write any more now," and that's the end of the letter.

Very close to my dugout was a theater which was underground, for soldiers to view movies, and they were showing *Going My Way* with Bing Crosby and I thought about going to the show, and then I thought, "No, I think I'll just stay here and write a letter to Mother."

A 155 millimeter shell dropped in about ten feet from my foxhole and I didn't know what to do. I was really in terrible shape. And I heard the moaning and groaning, the theater had been hit and a great number of kids were killed and wounded.

So I said, "Well, I've got to get out and help those guys." And so I started to get out, and bam,

another shell came in in the same spot. That did it. I stayed in that foxhole like a coward the whole night long, trembling. So I abandoned that foxhole and went forward to a bigger one where two or three of us slept closer to the front line. That was my antidote to what had happened.

I don't know if there's any dignity on the battlefield but I was trying to regain my composure and try to establish—I was battling myself. There was this terrible feeling.

And then I came back and I painted that morning. I said, "If I don't paint now, I'll never paint again, I'll never go to the front again." And so I painted the picture [p. 14] which I think is one of the strongest things I ever did, of these dazed soldiers picking up the debris and the clothes, and all that was left of the theater was this tree with no leaves on it. And so I painted these men with dazed looks, and clouds up above that seemed to reach like a dragon, like in the

Reep '44

Goya's *Disasters of War*. Everything seemed to be tragic, terrible, and meaningless.

We were up in the snow before Bologna. I brought back a painting. It was too cold to paint. I went into this dugout. It had two bunks in it. I brought back my painting and I placed this [painting] near a little wood furnace. I curled up with Somerset Maugham's *Of Human Bondage* by candlelight. And when I got up and I looked at my painting it was gone — there was a wet puddle on the dirt of the floor of my foxhole. It was so cold that the paint froze, and then next to the heater it melted, and my painting melted with it.

There was a fellow who hauled a bathtub out of Notuno [Italy], and he pulled it over near my foxhole. So I thought, "I'll paint a picture of him," [p. 17] because he filled that bathtub with water, and then he punched a hole in a gas tank and lit it. And would you believe that gasoline would drip on the ground a drop at a time, I was frightened to death at first. I thought the bathtub would blow up, this would be a hell of a way for me to go in the war.

The bathtub painting was nutty. That's all there was to it. How in the world could this man be smiling on a beachhead where shell fire would come all of the time, constantly. There he was smiling, taking a hot bath.

I was told that my painting of the soldier taking a bath was on the newsreel, and that Eleanor Roosevelt stood in front of it. What she said, I have no idea, but I know my parents and my family went to the movies all that week because in those days the *Movietone News* would be on every show.

I played a little tonette. It's a little plastic toy. How did that sound on the battlefield? In the foxholes there weren't any instruments, there weren't

Left: The Morning After

any radios. And when those tones, regardless of how shrill they were out of this little plastic toy, wafted over the battlefield you could feel them listening — creatures, this bizarre-looking battlefield was filled with these creatures, those of us who lived under the ground — only a direct hit would kill us, but we were frightened.

As you can see in the dugout painting [p.18] there's a fellow spreading a [canvas] shelter half. He's trying to get in, and we're crowded, because they wanted to be near the music. On the painting, of course, I tried to express the crowded nature of it. And I remember my lessons from a teacher of mine, who had taught us symbols of force. And I used them by having arrow forms come in on both sides to make them feel compressed. And then I pulled the guys' knees up to their chins in kind of distorted shapes.

I tried to create the sense of compression and also that sense of being frightened and yet being brave at the same time. And yet we were all waiting for the next shell. And there was shelling every single night. Every night. We just counted our blessings when we got up in the morning and weren't hit.

The proudest moment I ever had was when I saw that kid in the Anzio field have his leg blown off and I ran out into the field to help him. And I didn't know quite what to do, and an aid man came up in a jeep just after me. And the captain of the company that I was with was yelling at me, "Reep, Reep, come back here, come back here, come back," and I said, "The hell with him, I'm going out there and try to help this guy."

Well, that was, I thought, a very good act, and I was trying to vindicate myself for having stayed in that foxhole. And then when we were driving him to the hospital I was sitting in the back and we went over a bump and he was ice cold and I

Right: Soldier Bathing

said, "He's dead." And the guy opened his eyes. He says, "The hell I am!"

War is not a soldier strangling another soldier in a water-filled shell hole. That's a lot of hooey. All of those recreated pictures done by artists who imagined that this is what war is are crazy, because first of all, you wouldn't want to get close enough to strangle anybody. So the movies have given you exaggerated ideas about what war is all about.

There's nothing good about war. I can appreciate why [we went to war], especially after the Hitler regime — imagine slaughtering seven million people. I hated him, and it was my idea once I got into uniform to kill as many Nazis as possible. And when I finally had the opportunity to do it, I couldn't kill them, I just captured them, and a great number of them were half trying to surrender by the time I approached them.

I was asked to come down to see a colonel about staying in the Army, and I thought about it. He made it very tempting. He wanted to make me a major and send me to Austria for the Army of Occupation. And I looked at him and I kept looking at him and I kept looking at his mouth. It was very straight and stern, and he had steely gray eyes and clipped speech. "Captain Reep." And so I said, "God, no, I don't want to be a part of this any more." I said, "No, I want to go home. I don't want to be in the Reserve. I don't want to go over to Austria, I don't want to do anything. I just want to go home." And I was dismissed. And I was home.

I'd had so much war, there had been five years of the Army, and it just seemed that it consumed me. And I just couldn't go on with thinking war. I wanted peace and happiness and to live like other people.

Left: Dugout at Anzio

You get to the point where you say, why am I making pictures of what is real tragedy

for a lot of people back home and these wonderful boys who are wasted? And I'm mak-

ing pictures of them being wasted. It's hard to take.

Manuel Bromberg

—U.S. Army

I don't think for sure that I decided to be an artist. I had a very strong mother. I got out of art school in '37, I went to California because my mother was there. I did caricatures there on the boardwalk, on the Venice pier, and made a lot of money at ten cents or more a drawing. Once in my career I did caricatures on the backs of chorus girls, with grease paint. It was an act that I did for this casino when I was in art school.

When Pearl Harbor happened, the night before, I was in bed and I asked Jane to marry me. I was toying about enlisting right along because I was very upset about Hitler, but as soon as I found out Jane was pregnant, I didn't want to have any part of enlisting.

I wasn't drafted 'til April 15, 1942.

I had a marvelous colonel. This man had me decorating the whole camp. Called me in, I was only a private, and he said, "I know your work," he said, "Look at this camp, it's terrible. The men have to live in this situation. Would you help me out? I'll send you anywhere you want to go, let's decorate this place. Let's make it more livable." So I was doing huge murals, like five thousand square feet, on Service Club walls.

I had finished basic training and here was a letter from Washington telling me that I'd been appointed a war artist for whatever theater I wanted.

I picked India, Burma, and China and they said, "No, you can't, we're sending you to England."

Of course I was really excited, and if you could see this incredibly well-written commission where they describe what they expect of you, they wanted you to be like Goya.

What a heavy handle, what a thing to lay on you. [It read in part] "Dear Private Bromberg, You have been recommended by the War Department Art Advisory Board, as one of a small group of outstanding American artists, to go to an active war theater, and there to obtain a graphic record of the war." As Henry Varnum Poor, one of the best artists of that time, phrased it, "The United States must take the lead and find some way of getting from our finest artists and writers the things they alone can give—a deeply, passionately felt but profoundly reflective interpretation of the spirit and the essence of war."

It was an enormous opportunity. And if you're supposed to think [about] your interpretation of an event like a war, you know, you're not sure that you're the person to do it. I mean, who is really?

I found all through my two and a half years overseas that I was trying to find a way to describe this event called war.

When I was in London, the Luftwaffe was coming over and the bombs were falling. When you talk about people in combat, all the people of London were in combat. I mean, they were the

Above: Bromberg, Paris, France
Opposite Top: With Jane in Woodstock, NY, the day he asked her to marry him.
Opposite Bottom: Chalk Up Another

front lines when those bombs were dropping. You either stay where you are and get hit or you move to a shelter and on the way get hit.

I always drew a lot in London, the pubs and people. I was always interested in people. It's more Daumier for me, I mean gestural relationships of moments.

If you look at Air Force paintings, you see hydraulics, you see wings, you see mechanical things nicely rendered, you know? But it doesn't tell you much, it's a very difficult subject.

One of the big problems was the color. Everything is OD. You know, olive drab. And think of it, the uniforms, the weaponry, it's all generally the same color.

I was assigned to the final dress rehearsal for the D-Day invasion, down the rope ladders into the assault boats. It was a little similar to what turned out to be Omaha Beach.

But the exercises—everything worked so beautifully, you know? Heavy equipment got ashore. Nothing at all like what happened later.

I was excited about the invasion. If it was anything like Slapton Sands [Southeast England], it's gonna be—yes! A very exciting thing! But then it wasn't like Slapton Sands, was it?

These boys are eighteen and they are superbly trained, beautiful guys. They were marvelous young men. At twenty-five, I was an old man compared to them.

My assignment was Omaha Beach. And my boat position would bring me into the beach twenty minutes after the first hit. That would be H-hour plus twenty minutes.

But Sir Kenneth Clark, who was in charge of all the British war artists, said to my commanding officer, "How can you send Bromberg in? I'm not letting any of my artists go in until D+ thirty days. And you're sending him in twenty minutes after the first hit, on the beach. And what good will that do you? You only have three artists and you're gonna have two." And so they

Above: "Woman and Child—Normandy"
Right: Soldiers Resting

rescinded my boat position. If I had gone with my boat position, I would be dead.

I knew these people who were almost 100 percent casualties there on the beach.

This moment in the life of — or death of — these young men, they're on the verge of not coming back. They're descending into a kind of hell. It's going into a 100 percent chance of casualty, in this case because they're going into Omaha Beach and these are people of the 116th. The whole thing was terribly sad, wasteful, and heroic, all at the same time.

But the beach itself, as far as you could see, was the biggest, biggest junkyard in the world. I've no other way to express it. There were ships beached. There was debris everywhere you looked. Barbed wire, boats, bodies were still floating from the original hit.

I was very innocently going around looking for visual things. I spent days on that beach.

And then they would move inland with an assignment. And at one point I went all the way into Cherbourg and it seems like I went through no man's land. I didn't know it. I went through an area that we hadn't really captured yet.

And when I got to Cherbourg, at a German headquarters, their food was still on the table in the mess hall. They were that recently out of there.

The historical section finally moved lock, stock, and barrel out of London to Paris.

I wanted to go to Paris. I had convinced my su-

Above: German Surrenders
Opposite, top: LST Grounded
Opposite, bottom: "Soldier with duffel on gangway"

periors that I would rather be given a bayonet and a gun and given the best equipment to be an infantryman. Otherwise, if I was gonna be the war artist, they had to give me my own studio.

Until then, in London, we didn't have such a convenience. So [in Paris] they gave me the Austrian Embassy. I had French windows looking out on the Rue Vaugennes, off the Avenue Hoche. There were other artists there, too. And it was beautiful. I was right off the Arc de Triomphe. Once we got to France I visited Picasso, I visited Bracque. Of course the most exciting visit was to Picasso's studio. And at that time, to see Picasso was not easy.

And I was floored, not only by Picasso, but by what I saw, because I never have seen so many art supplies in an artist's studio.

I was dizzy with this stuff.

The big advantage of being an artist was I could meet poor working people, I could meet the Comtesse de Neuilly, I could meet Communists, I could meet middle-income people. That's the advantage of being in art...I was acceptable on all sides.

So, while I'm here in Paris waiting on an as-

Above: Bromberg (left) with Olin Dows (middle) and Pablo Picasso (right)

Right: The Card Players

signment, the war is going on toward Germany. And so I'm drawing models, and I'm working on my paintings, developing some paintings from sketches.

Toward the end of the war, I really didn't want to do any more pictures. I could go wherever I was assigned and know that I was going to be able to leave and go back to London or Paris, whereas most [soldiers] couldn't. So I got to this point where I just didn't want to make any more art on the subject, it's that kind of guilt.

You're using their misery or their death or this wreckage for subject matter for your art.

I came home to a daughter who was almost three and a half years old. And married life, and peacetime. And I couldn't adjust to peacetime. I noticed that all the bridges were standing, because everywhere you're looking [in Europe], the bridges are down.

I think I had done about 150 paintings that were sent back to Washington. Everything I did was taken from me. I couldn't even tear up things that I didn't like. It was property of the Army. I was really very unhappy about everything I did, but I had an exhibit not too long ago and suddenly I said, "They're not too bad."

Right: "Wounded/Dying Soldier"

Bromberg
E.TO. 6/44

Essay

Chaos of Combat

In order to put the viewer squarely into the middle of combat — the confusion of it, the sound, the smell — the artist had little choice but to put himself squarely into the middle of it. He went to the front lines and through his art, he made sense of it for us. He showed us war's awful hideousness and its compelling beauty. He also showed us history.

Opposite: Cornwell, Detail of *Anti-Aircraft Crew in Action*

Above: Benney, *The Battle of Midway*
Below: Cornwell, *Anti-Aircraft Crew in Action*
Opposite: Pleissner, *Sherman Tank*
Overleaf: Lea, *Explosion*

Above: Davis, *Hamburg Raid*
Below: Lea, *The Price*
Right: Millman, *Wet Landing*

Above: Rigg, *Armor and Atom*
Below: Fischer, *The Campbell*

Above: Eby, *Fighting on Tarawa*
Below: Eby, *Night Work*

Above: Dickson, *Here It Comes*
Below: Eby, *Ebb Tide*
Right: Reep, *Anzio Harbor*

Above: Coale, *The Japanese Attack of Pearl Harbor*
Below: Shepler, *Kamikaze Attack*
Opposite: Benney, *Death of the Shoho*

Above: Sample, *Dawn Patrol of Launching*
Opposite, top: Jamieson, *Invasion Craft—Sicily*
Opposite, bottom: Jamieson, *Kamerad*

Above: Dickson, *Battle Scene*
Below: Eby, *Jungle*
Opposite, top: Von Ripper, *Soldiers Killed in the Rapido River Xing*
Opposite, bottom: Lavalle, *Coning Searchlights*

Marines' Best Friend

The Marine Corps Combat Correspondent Program

These men are not artists in Marine Corps uniform. They are Marines who can paint and sketch and can find time, or are given time, to do so. They wear the uniform because they have earned the right to wear it, just as has every Marine. They are Marines first, and artists, or anything else, second. This is in strict line with the tradition of the Corps: Every man a fighting man.

—Brigadier General Robert L. Denig, U.S.M.C., 1943

The combat artist became an integral part of the U.S. Marine Corps thanks to a visionary "combat correspondent" program that was developed in the early days of World War II. Brigadier General Robert L. Denig became the Director of Public Relations for the United States Marine Corps shortly before Pearl Harbor. A veteran Marine with thirty-six years of active duty in the Corps, Denig brought enthusiasm and energy to the office. When war was declared, he had a vision of recruiting young writers and photographers to be Marine correspondents in the field. It was only a short time before this concept would be expanded to include artists. Sent into battle like any other Marines, they would be uniquely qualified to write—or capture in pictures—compelling and authentic stories about Marine activity.

Denig was given permission from Major General Commandant Thomas Holcomb to recruit ten reporters and photographers for combat duty, with the promise that if he was successful, he could recruit more. Denig and his officers were so good at selling the idea that there was soon a shortage of young reporters in Washington. Cissie Herald, the owner of the *Washington Times Herald,* went so far as to complain to President Roosevelt about the nine young journalists who left her newsroom to become combat correspondents. General Holcomb ordered Denig to look for new recruits elsewhere.

The Associated Press ran this announcement about the program in June, 1942:

Lieutenant General Thomas A. Holcomb, commandant of the United States Marine Corps, announced today that newspaper reporters of not less than five years experience are being accepted for enlistment as combat correspondents. After six weeks training as fighting troops, they will be given the rank of sergeant and sent overseas with combat units. General Holcomb said the Marine Corps is sacrificing none of its high standards, and combat correspondents must meet all physical requirements of regular Marines.

Opposite: Dickson, *Marines' Best Friend*

The first artist to be recruited to work under Denig was Hugh Laidman, who was recommended by a fellow Marine Corps officer who had admired his artwork. Soon a good number of artists were working alongside the Marine Corps combat correspondents. Denig was quick to advocate the unique role of the artist in bringing the impact of war to the American public.

> Art at any time is food for spiritual growth. The centuries have proved it so. At peace or at war, man cannot live by bread alone. A special case for art in time of war may be made, for it is then that man's spiritual, as well as physical, being is most severely in need of sustaining strength. Whatever provides the people good cheer, material for reflection, and inspiration is an essential contribution to a nation's total effort.
>
> This is a people's war. The people want to know, need to know, and have a right to know, what is going on.

Many artists, like Dick Gibney, volunteered for the program with the hope of putting their artistic skills to use on the battlefield. None were spared the trials of Marine Corps recruit training. Before they were allowed to be artists, they had to become Marines.

Parris Island boot camp was tough. Many of the combat correspondents later felt that the rigorous training

Opposite: Hios, *Ambush at Saipan*

52

appeared in the nation's leading magazines and newspapers, often accompanied by a gallery showing of the original art. The National Gallery mounted a show of Marine combat art in November 1943.

Many of the Marine combat artists were fresh from art school—the noted artist Harry Jackson was only nineteen at the time. Others were quite old to be on the front lines. Experienced World War I combat artist and nationally known muralist George Harding fought and painted in practically every battle area of World War II for the Marine Corps.

Marines with artistic talent often drew as a recreation or to entertain their buddies. Some artists were plucked from the ranks of the corps to become combat correspondents by the Division of Public Relations. Young Victor Donahue, for example, came to their attention by drawing cartoons on the faces of envelopes that his fellow Marines sent home to their girlfriends.

they endured there saved their lives on the battlefield. Denig's philosophy from the beginning was that the artists, as enlisted men themselves, would be better able to understand and depict the experience of enlisted men at war. Each correspondent, he wrote, "learned to drill, to deploy for attack, to use his bayonet, to fire basic weapons, to walk guard watches, to serve always with a high degree of discipline and durability."

The first Marine combat correspondents went overseas in August 1942 to posts all over the world, from Londonderry to Iceland, Alaska to Jamaica. Very soon Marine combat art was being shipped home to Denig depicting the action in Dutch Harbor, Rendova, and Guadalcanal. It

The artwork was produced under extreme conditions. In a Marine landing, the artist was expected to fight like any other Marine until the beach was secured. He would take cover and make sketches during the heat of the battle, but he would usually complete his work in the rear echelons, after the fighting stopped. Always the artist tried to communicate the truth of his experience. Donald Dickson, one of the best known Marine artists, said, "I'm not interested in drawing Marines who are spick and span and smartly dressed. I don't want to gloss over life out here. It's dirty and hot and rugged and that's the way I want to draw it."

General Denig realized that these interpretations of what a Marine had just witnessed and lived through gave the artist some advantages over the combat photographer:

The combat photographer must snap his picture of an action as it happens. If he is busy taking part in the action, as he so often is; if it happens so fast he is unable to adjust his camera in time; if conditions are not good, the action is never recorded—and the picture is never made.

The artist, on the other hand, with his photographic eye, can take part in the action, and then paint any moment of it from memory at his leisure.

The painter can provide his own lighting; he can give a picture any degree of intensity he desires. He can reconstruct a scene from whatever angle he considers most dramatic, centering attention wherever he wishes.

The Marine Corps collection from World War II represents a rough, intimate, and some-

times startlingly beautiful account of Marines at war. Today the artwork is housed in the Marine Corps Museum at the Washington Navy Yard in Washington, D.C. The collection is curated by Mr. John T. Dyer. Dyer was inspired in his youth by the combat art from World War II. He himself painted and sketched as a Marine in Vietnam.

Above: Donahue, *Crash Crew Member*
Opposite: Dunn, *It was Dark and Wet, Bougainville*

I enlisted with the Marines with a vague kind of promise from the recruiting sergeant

that yes, the Marines did have use for an artist.

Richard Gibney

—U.S. Marines

What I had was this map case. In here was my sketchbooks and paper, I had bottles of ink in there, pencils, and other things. And this is carried by a strap over my shoulder, along with my other equipment. I was armed, like any Marine, with an M-1 rifle and a .38 pistol, a bayonet, a K-bar knife, ammunition around my waist and across my chest.

It had this ratty strap here…and boy, this is sure going to hell and gone.

The day of leaving home—that's kind of a traumatic thing for a young fella that hadn't been that far away from home before.

I know the day that I had to leave I was quite fearful. I'd heard stories about the Marine Corps that'd curl your hair. I was afraid of it.

And yet I knew that was the place where perhaps I could do my best art.

I had been assigned to a marine brigade and a representative from the engineers battalion arrived and said they were looking for volunteers for the engineers. And it occurred to me that maybe they would be responsible for the camouflaging of buildings and vehicles, and they said yes, they were. And I said, "Oh, I've got some art training—maybe that would be a place where I could utilize some of my knowledge of color and so on." "Oh, yeah, we'd love to have you! Have your seabag packed, fall out." And so I did and we were taken to another part of the island.

And I heard those ominous words when we stopped, "Assault Engineers, assemble here!" And my name was one of the first. Ah, that word, "Assault"! It turned out there would be a modicum of camouflage taught, but I was to be trained primarily as a demolition man.

We moved from pill box to pill box and shell hole to shell hole. The noise was terrible. It was like a huge storm going on. And the air was filled with white coral dust, it looked like a snowstorm. It got into your hair, under your helmet. It got inside your clothes. It was like having sandpaper rubbing against your skin. I can remember my ankles were bleeding from walking around in that stuff. There were areas where to move ahead you had to walk over bodies.

I would try to do sketches when they'd say, "Okay, fall out"; we'd always have a chance for rest. And in the evening I would write my letters, but I would also make sketches. I found out that I was in demand to do portraiture. Guys would want me to do their girlfriend from a photograph.

And one day at my tent door my company commander appeared, a man respected very much, Captain Bransom, he said, "Gibney, get all your drawings together and meet me in front of the company office." So, gee, I scrambled and got all the drawings I had together and went around to the company office. He appeared there and said, "Get in the jeep." And I swung my legs in, and he said, "We're going to division headquarters, I want

in the drawings I had. He spread them out on his desk and he said, "You know that First Division and Third Division have got more than one artist in their outfit." He said, "We don't have any, you're going to fill the bill for us. And I want to take these drawings, if you'll let me, and I'll send them back to Washington to General Denig's office." And I said, "Sure."

About three weeks later the appointment came out of Washington that I was the official combat artist of that division. So they said, "Now, you fill your map case up," this one here, "with sharpened pencils and razor blades and lots of paper and whatever you need, because you're going to draw and paint from now on."

Oh, I was excited.

I made sketches. Those are the things I would

you to show these drawings you've been doing to Captain Louis Hayward, he's the public relations officer there." And so we drove over, I met Captain Hayward, who seemed to be very interested

make while I was with the unit, or as soon as I

Above: Leaving Home (Odyssey)
Below: Richard Gibney

58

could after a landing. You can't say, "Hold the war, I'm drawing you." But you take cover. When you get a chance, you think you can stick your head up enough to see what's going on, you make some quick sketches, try to find a better place to be where you can do more of that.

I think one good thing that us artists should always have is a damn good memory.

I was on deck sketching and drawing the scenes in the harbor around me. There were some battleships there and cruisers. And a friend came by, he said, "Come on, Gib, we're going forward to play some Hearts now." He and I always played Hearts when we were at sea. And this time I said, "No, I'll see you guys later. I want to finish what I'm doing. I gotta finish this drawing I'm making." And so he said, "Well, OK, we'll be up forward on the elevator deck." A short time after that, while I was drawing, the whole front end of that ship blew up. A huge sheet of flame burst into the air, and it sucked the air right out of my lungs.

And it came back together again around my head, I went deaf after that, and it knocked me down. Blew my shirt right off of me. And it came right up through where those guys were playing cards. And the fact that I didn't go, I guess, is why I'm still here. I've often wondered why I was always one jump ahead of something.

In moments of dire emergency, if our backs were to the sea, I was to act like a Marine. Having experienced it, that's one of the things that the Marine Corps had about their combat correspondents, be they writers, artists, or photographers, was that they were going to be more

Above: Assault Engineers

effective in expressing what they do if they are also Marines sharing in it. So it often occurred to me, how could I have attempted to show what it was like if I hadn't done it? It wouldn't have been authentic.

One of the generals asked, "Don't we have enough photographers? What do you need artists for?" But the artist brought another viewpoint that was impossible any other way. They thought it was necessary to have artists, photographers, and writers, all three of us. And it made sense to me.

Without artists we probably would have a lesser understanding, even of our own American Revolution.

On Saipan, we would have to go out on these incessant patrols, day after day, to clear out rag-tag groups of armed Japanese that refused to surrender, even after the island was secured. It was a dangerous place. I would fall asleep at night

and kind of hope I didn't wake up, and that I wouldn't have to do that again.

You know that sheer hell is going on on that is-land [Tarawa]. You can see it. You can hear it. It rolls over the water. You can hear that thunder. And then the word comes from the bridge, "All Marines go down to your debarkation stations." Your heart flutters. And it's amazingly quiet. There isn't a lot of shouting and talking and hub-bub. The kind of control you have to have over yourself, all these men have that. So they're keeping their innermost fears quiet. They don't express them. They show concern for each other. That impressed me.

I, being a good Irish Catholic, made the sign of the cross. And I had to put my foot over that rail-ing. That is when you want to . . . you're saying Hail Marys but you want to throw up, too. You'd give anything if you could go the other way. But you

Above: At Sea, Purple Clouds

60

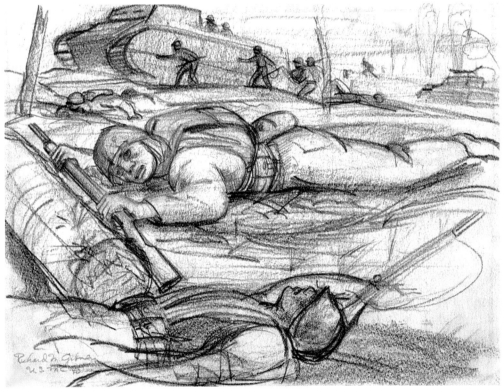

Above: Over the Side
Below: Sketch of dead soldiers

Above, left: Soldiers boarding troop ship
Above, right: Sketch of landing craft
Below: Tarawa Landing
Opposite: Down the Nets

know you have to go, you have to go down. And you beg the good Lord to see you through it and to please let you see home again. And then there's that thick rope under your foot and as you go down that net, you have to be aware of people below you, preceding you. You don't want to step on them. You don't want somebody to step on you. A couple of times you feel a foot on your hand. You're carrying a lot of weight. The pack is probably a good sixty, sixty-five pounds and biting into your shoulders.

You've got your rifle over your shoulder slapping against you as you go down. You tie your helmet so that it won't fall off at that point. Your muscles are aching. Your insides are full of fear as you make your way down that net. And the main sounds are not voices, they're just the sounds of equipment. But you make your way down the side of the ship and it seems to be down the side of a tall building, those boats that you're heading for are far below. And they're riding up and down, probably ten feet or more [p. 63].

If I thought we saw chaos before, this was even worse. I can't tell you the number of bodies of American Marines that were lying facedown in the water.

I have one painting of that. And I thought long and hard about it when I made the painting, "Should I show how many there were? Well, no, I'd need a big canvas for that." So I thought, "One says it all for all of them," so I did one body. And I call it *The Last Full Measure*.

We left so many out there.

To see an American Marine lying dead with a bullet in his head was enraging. We knew that we had to dominate that island.

The further we got into that war, the sheer and utter waste of it...I don't ever want to go to war again. I know the world probably will, but I hope it doesn't. But if it can be done without the blood flowing, so much the better. I'd prefer that. Part of what I'm trying to say is that one of my favorite paintings is *The Last Full Measure*. Here's a young American lying facedown in the water, who is there because he's defending some principles, and what a sad thing that he had to go that far to do it. I think these are the things that artists think about.

We used to think, "Oh, God, maybe we'll be home in a year." Well, a year comes and goes, and people talk about eighteen months. We couldn't imagine anybody being gone eighteen months. And eighteen months goes by and you're into two years, and you're into three years. You forget about going home after a while. Home becomes very faint and distant in your memory.

One painting I never made, and I wish I had because I still see it today, we had a burial at sea and they had a flag over them. The Catholic chaplain said some words, and then they were taken to the rail and tipped. You could hear it slide, sloop, and then the splash. I thought, "I hope that never happens to me."

People wonder why you're an artist, "You're much too sensitive, what were you doing in the Marine Corps? Did you do these drawings and these paintings from photographs?" And I would have to tell them, "No, I was there. I was a Marine like any other Marine." And as a result, I was scared to death. The fear, you're so trained as a Marine not to give in to that, you're part of a team, your fellow Marines are your concern. The success of the campaign is your concern. So there's tremendous personal discipline you have to exercise in order to achieve this, but that doesn't say that you're not feeling the most terrible anguish and fear inside. The fight is to not give in to it. And the other fight is to find cover.

The last painting on my easel I'm having trouble finishing now because I'm legally blind. If you look at another human being or a child, there's a wonderful look in an eye, the smile that may have a complexion that seems to mirror some kind of inner purity. I can't see that any longer.

Above: On Deck

Opposite: The Last Full Measure

Essay

The Artist's Eye

Each artist made a conscious decision about what he chose to paint and draw. This was war as he saw it. This was his war. Though we have a strong sense of what World War II looked like though newsreels and iconographic photographs, no camera was big enough or sentient enough to take into its embrace the startling out-of-placeness of a plasma bottle pegged to a palm tree, or the contradiction of a GI with flowers springing from his helmet, or the puzzlement of children contemplating the bloody scrappings outside a surgeon's tent.

Opposite: Sample, Detail of *Delirium is Our Best Deceiver*

Above: Boggs, "Porters and Soldiers Carrying Equipment"
Opposite, top: Benney, *Just off the Line*
Opposite, bottom: Smith, *Normandy Wash*

Above: Craig, Monte Cassino

Above: Von Ripper, *French Infantry*

Below: Sample, *Delirium is Our Best Deceiver*

Above: Von Ripper, *Murdered Rape Victims in Woods of Italy*
Opposite, top: Boggs, *Sea Island Paradise*
Opposite, bottom: Reep, *Pack Train*

Above: Boggs, *An Emotion of War*
Opposite, top: Thomas, *Dock Area*
Opposite, bottom: Davis, *After They've Gone*

The Face of War

The portraits painted by the combat artists are more than pictures drawn from life. They are as much pictures of war. We see it in the dazed faces of men who fought, in eyes that have lost their light and in mouths that have forgotten what it is to smile.

Soldiers — ordinary Joes — were willing subjects. At times, the drawings were theirs to keep. These portraits were sent home from "somewhere in Europe" or "somewhere in the Pacific." For many families, it would be the last likeness of a son or husband.

Opposite: Lea, *General Chennault*

Above: Lea, *Thousand Yard Stare*
Opposite, top: Lea, *Going In, Peleiu, 1944*
Opposite, bottom: Reep, *We Move Again*

Above: Draper, Adm. William F. Halsey
Below: Brodie, *Corpsman*
Right: Hirsch, *The Burden*

Above: L.B. Smith, *The Man Without a Gun*

Above: Eby, *Portrait of a Young Bomber*

Above: Arnest, *Two Soldiers*
Opposite, top: Murray, *Lt. Col. John L. Smith*
Opposite, bottom: Hurd, *Aerial Gunner*

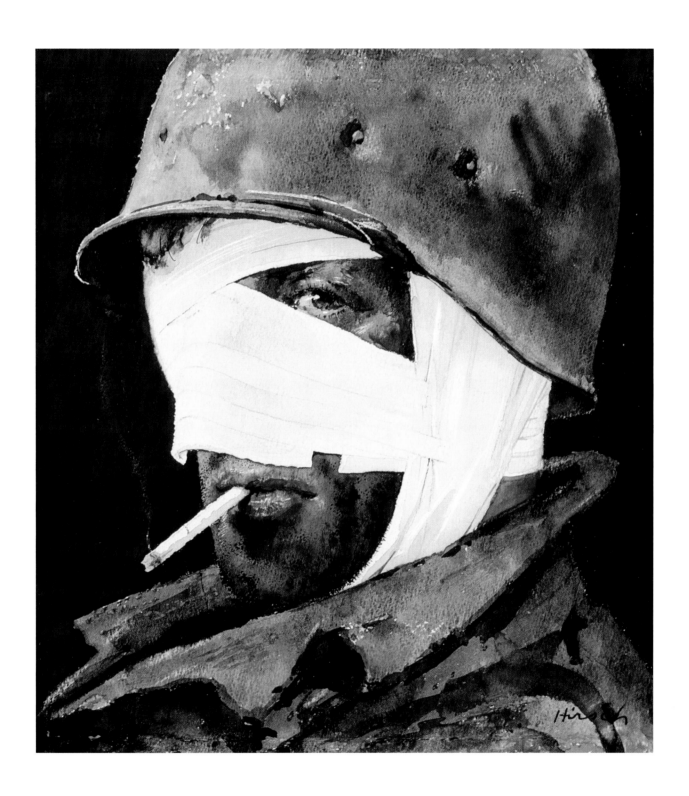

Above: Hirsch, *Hi Visibility Wrap*

Opposite, top: Eby, *Marine Marksman*

Opposite, bottom, left to right: Whitcomb, *Smiling Wave;* Jamieson, *Johnny;* Brodie, *Pfc. Joe Esz*

Navy Art Program

I would willingly give my life and the knowledge of a lifetime to have a chance to make such records for our people.

—Griffith Baily Coale, USNR

On March 11, 1941, Franklin D. Roosevelt's lend-lease act became law, enabling the U.S. to transfer munitions to the Allies. Many Americans were certain that this spelled imminent U.S. involvement in the global conflict. A week after the announcement, Griffith Baily Coale, a New York artist well-known for his murals, wrote the Navy with a proposal.

> As I am an artist who has made a life-time study of maritime lore, as well as historical research ... and as I am a small boat sailor and thorough lover of the sea and ships, I would like to offer my services to my country by applying for a commission as a reserve officer in the United States Navy. I propose to make paintings from sketches and drawings ashore and afloat of ships, yards, docks, and all the intricacies incorporated in the running of a mighty navy.

Coale had a vision of emulating an arrangement between the British Royal Navy and several prominent artists during World War I. He believed that the Navy should commission "officer artists" and send them into battle to make a historical record that could also be used in the

Navy's public relations campaign. The British World War I art was so exciting, he argued, that reproductions had even been published in a recent issue of *Life*.

Coale's dream became a reality with more speed and drama than he had probably envisioned. In August he was commissioned as Lieutenant Commander and assigned to accompany a convoy to Iceland in waters prowled by German submarines. He made a diary of his experiences to accompany his paintings. On October 31, the destroyer *Reuben James* was torpedoed and sunk off western Iceland with a loss of about one hundred men, the first U.S. naval vessel to be lost by enemy action, and Coale was there to witness it.

Convinced by the play given to Coale's paintings of the *Reuben James* disaster by many national U.S. magazines, the Art and Poster Section of the Navy Department's Office of Public Relations set out to commission several other carefully selected artists. They would be sent out as officer-artists on combat assignments. Captain Leland P. Lovette, director of Public Relations, outlined the official thinking behind this decision.

> Painters ... could catch the dramatic intensity of a scene and put it down on canvas. They could also omit the confi-

Opposite: Coale, *Sinking of the* Reuben James

dential technical details which a camera might reveal, thus making many interesting subjects available for publication. Subjects beyond the range of photography can be vividly depicted by painters, such as action at night, or in foul weather, or action widely scattered over the sea or in the air.

Four artists were selected for this position. William Draper, Albert Murray, and Dwight Shepler—artists who had already enrolled in the Navy for general duties—were transferred to public relations and dubbed official "officer-artists." Mitchell Jamieson was recruited from New York.

The Navy artists had to earn their officer status. They went through deck officer training and were assigned to stand watch while at sea. Like any other sailor, they took their proper turn at regular duties aboard ship. Sketching and photography on board was confined to off hours. Said Captain Lovette, "In this way the artists obtain a better and more thorough understanding of their subject matter and are able to render it more convincingly."

The officer-artists reported to the commander or a given fleet or unit armed with art supplies and letters of introduction from the Department of Public Affairs. But, like the Army and Marine programs, they

Left: Jamieson, *Burial Ground*

were more or less responsible for organizing their time and choosing their own subject matter once in the field. They would occasionally be called upon to render other services that called upon their skill as artists, such as observing color conditions to aid in camouflage, or drawing charts and identification silhouettes.

Dwight Shepler was the first artist to enter a combat zone. He was sent to Hawaii, where he was able to meet with Admiral Nimitz, who gave his blessing to the project. Shepler witnessed his first action in the Battle of Santa Cruz aboard the USS *San Juan*. Upon leaving his battle station, he would make sketches and notes of the action he had just witnessed—Japanese torpedo

planes attacking, U.S. ships set ablaze. When the fighting was over, Shepler finished paintings of the battle and sent them to Washington. He was soon on the ground covering the action of the Marines in Guadalcanal.

The other officer-artists worked on their own interpretations of the historic events taking place in combat zones around the world. Lt. William Draper was sent to the Aleutians, where he painted the Japanese attacks at Amchitka. Lt. Albert Murray was sent to the Caribbean Naval bases after some harrowing experiences on the USS *Boise*, and Mitchell Jamieson was in North Africa prior to taking part in the invasion of Sicily.

Artistic interpretations of war flowed from the

Above: Shepler, *Under the Enemy's Nose*
Opposite: Hoffman, *First Aid to the Fallen*

pencils and brushes of many other enlisted men throughout the Navy. Some of these men were appointed combat artists in the field, sanctioned by their commanding officers to paint in their off hours. Their artwork reveals an intimate and comprehensive portrait of the Navy at war — portraits of the men the artists lived and fought with every day; action rendered expressively by men who witnessed it.

Several Navy officer-artists were present for the D-Day invasion at Omaha Beach. Mitchell Jamieson and Dwight Shepler were assigned to battleships that took part in the fighting during the first days of the invasion, eventually landing on the beach themselves. Shepler was subsequently transferred back to the Pacific, and he continued to paint for the remainder of the war, despite extreme exhaustion.

The Navy Collection from World War II comprises over six thousand pieces of artwork. The art is housed at the Navy Art Gallery at the Navy Yard in Washington, D.C.

When the war started, I wanted to get in the Navy to do something for my country.

William Draper

— U.S. Navy

I found that because I was nearsighted and I was 3-A that I didn't have a chance of getting into the service. So I decided to go and volunteer my services, and asked if I could do anything for the war effort, that I was an artist — and lo and behold they needed me. They wanted me to draw submarine wakes so that the planes could see the shape of the wake behind and know how far down the submarine was.

When I got to Washington I found that in a week I was going to be sent up to the Aleutians as an artist and it was a terrible time, there were terrible storms going on all that fall. Except I found a violet blooming up on a mountain in November, which was amazing to me. One of the worst things about my job was the weather. We had terrible weather, particularly in the Aleutians.

I remember painting in this blizzard, and I had my canvas set up and was painting the scene there, and suddenly this wind came up and gravel came up and stuck on my canvas and then [the canvas] wheeled off into the wind, and I went searching for it and found it on a woodpile and I left it like it was and it's there now in the Navy Department all plastered with gravel and grit and it looks like a storm, all this stuff going across the canvas.

I was about eleven and we went for lunch at the Boston Navy Yard on the Tennessee and after lunch Mother said, "William dear, will you play the piano for the officers?" and I played a Chopin waltz. And that was the end of that, except years later, I was probably twenty-nine, I had orders to go to the landing at Saipan on the Tennessee, so they roll the piano out on deck, and I played and sang on the same ship that I'd been on and played the piano on when I was eleven years old.

The enlisted men enjoyed my piano playing because I played the things they would like to hear. I played boogie woogie, which was very popular then — which I learned from Leonard Bernstein — and I played "Lydia the Tattooed Lady."

I was in this little boat, and we came alongside of this transport [ship], and they threw a little rope ladder down the side for me to get up. Well, I'd never been taught how to climb a rope ladder. I grabbed it, but I grabbed the last rung of the ladder. And I never could chin myself anyway, and there I was hanging on the side of the transport and I thought, "My God, if I let go, I'll drop into the propeller." I let go, finally, when I saw the little boat under me, and I dropped about fifteen feet into the boat. Then this great cargo net came over the side, and I just stuck myself through it like toothpicks, and they pulled me up. But that was the most narrow escape I think I ever had, I would have been dead if I had let go and the boat hadn't been there...

I was sent to Guam. I was on a flagship and somebody asked me, "Draper, where are you going to be during the battle?" And I said, "Oh,

I'll be on a destroyer a thousand yards out, watching the operation." And he said, "Oh, you're not gonna see anything out there. Why don't you come with me, I'm leading the assault troops in a sub-chaser." And I said, "Do you think I'll see it any better there?" Then he said, "Oh, yes, you'll see it better." Well, I went on the sub-chaser [and we headed in].

I got very excited, and in a moment of madness, when we were going in to shore, well, I had a .38 pistol, which I fired in the air, probably hit a Marine — no, I don't think I did, but I had the gun, and I thought I ought to shoot something. I got to shore, and I ran, and there was a hole in the ground with a little place I could squat down in. I forgot all my painting material in the landing boat.

After we had landed there, it was maybe the first week, I was sketching and painting and there were so many dead people there that we had to stop all activity and bury the dead. And I was watching them taking these bodies up and putting them in command cars and hauling them away and flopping them into a big hole and covering them up. I would weep over the ones that had crew haircuts. I was heartbroken when I saw the crew haircuts because that reminded me of my friends [at Harvard] somehow.

In the painting of the submarine tender I have

Above: The Landing
Opposite, top: Tired Tigers
Opposite, bottom: William Draper

four men working on a submarine, but it's only one man. I asked this guy if he would pose for me. He had a nice back, and I couldn't ask everybody to pose, so I got him to lean over and pose at one place. Then I had him pose in another position. I have him in four different positions in the picture, and I used him a lot.

While I was an official combat artist in the Navy, I was walking down a corridor in the Navy Department, and I overheard these two commanders talking. I wasn't listening, but the door was ajar, and I heard them say, "But Draper's not a portrait painter." I walked in and said, "My name's Draper, and I *am* a portrait painter." And so they said, "Well, we want you to paint Halsey and Nimitz when you're out in the Pacific." So, sure enough, I got Halsey and Nimitz both to pose for me, and that was a great thing to happen, because I'll tell you, it really made me — it was great for my reputation as a portrait painter,

Above: Admiral Chester W. Nimitz, USN
Left: Saipan

Above: Pilots at Play, Unak Alaska
Opposite, top: Richard Nixon
Opposite, bottom: John F. Kennedy

because Halsey and Nimitz were shown at the Metropolitan and shown in Washington at the National Gallery.

And that's a true story, believe it or not. I frankly have to say, I think it helped my career a great deal, because they were portraits, and I'm a portrait painter now. All because of Halsey and Nimitz, I think I can say. So you see, it's fate. Fate, fate, fate.

You know, I was an officer in the Navy, and the enlisted men all were terribly nice to me. For instance, they would help me carry my easel and my paintbox. One time in Guadalcanal I saw this orchid up in this tree and I wanted it very much so one of the enlisted men said, "Oh, I'll get that for you, sir, if you do a portrait of my wife in the nude from this snapshot. I said, "Well, great," so I took this snapshot and I copied it but left all the clothes off. It was a great hit, I loved doing it and I liked the picture, and he was crazy about it. This is what happened out there with all the men without women, I guess.

He had climbed the tree, brought the orchid down, and it was a dendrobium, beautiful white orchid. For years I haven't talked about it. I'm so surprised, and rather pleased, now that I'm being asked questions about it, 'cause I've sort of forgotten that I was a combat artist. And nobody seems to realize or to know that I was, today. I painted Nixon, which hangs in the National Portrait Gallery. I painted Kennedy, which is in the White House, and I painted the Shah of Iran for his coronation.

I painted so many people, and I'm so glad that I did, it's been very fascinating to me. I've enjoyed it, and hope they enjoyed me. I certainly made them have fun—I tell them limericks and things. I'll tell you one limerick: "There was a young girl named Bianca / Who slept while the sloop was at anchor / She awoke in dismay when she heard the mate say / We should pull up the top sheet and spank her." That's a good one, isn't it?

Do you want any more?

101

Diverse Visions

More than one hundred combat artists were assigned to document and interpret the war. They were recruited from all over the country. Their backgrounds were as different as night and day. Some had sophisticated art training, others had little. And they worked in every imaginable medium — some of their own invention. The range of their work was remarkable. Their artistic styles are a kaleidoscope of visual expression.

In their disparateness, they were of one mind — that war is as much a conflict of passion as it is of force.

Opposite: Lawrence, Detail of *Going Home*

Above: Von Ripper, *Crossing the Voltura Near Caiazzo*
Opposite, top: Lawrence, *Going Home*
Opposite, bottom: Benton, *Score Another for the Subs*

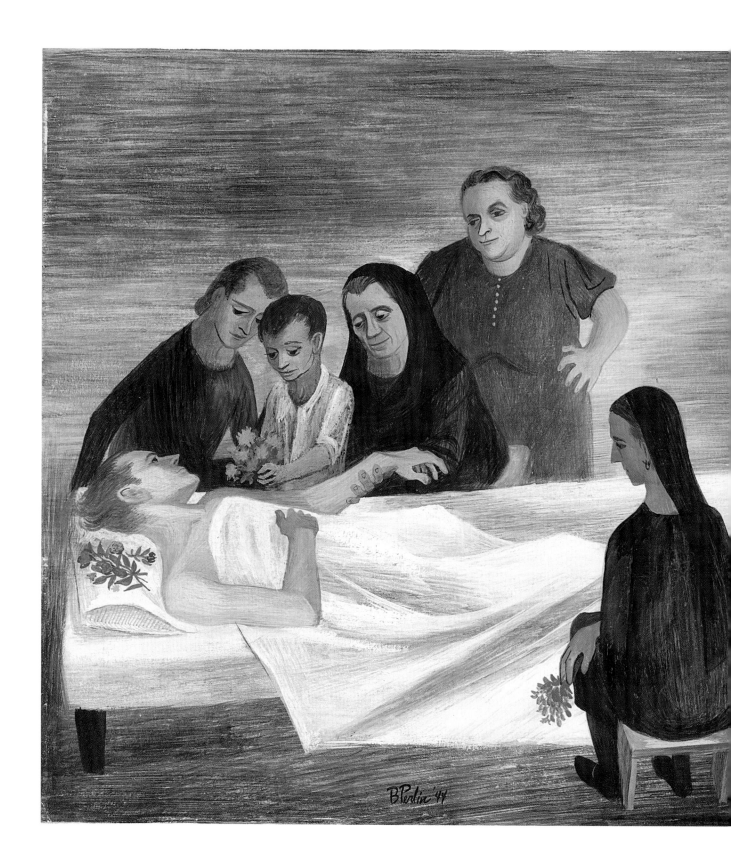

Above: Perlin, *At Bedside*

Above: Dunn, "Dead Japanese Soldiers"
Below: Sheets, *Bread Line*
Opposite, top: Kadish, *Three Dead Chinese Soldiers*
Opposite, bottom: Fredenthal, *Taking Cover*

Above: Siporin, *New Year's Day*
Below: Craig, *Bone Pile at Cassino*
Opposite: Schreiber, *Up Periscope*

Above: Reep, *Bombing of the Abbey*
Below: Biddle, *Dead Civilians*
Left: Sheahan, *Buchenwald*

Life Magazine War Art

In this war the artist is on the spot. Whatever his previous preoccupation with three plums in a silver dish or three girls in a grassy glade, the artist has now been wrenched out of it by the necessity of recording, under every imaginable human stress and terror, man's reaction to the greatest crises of all history. There may have been better artists than those who chanced to be born at this juncture in the world's affairs, but no artists have ever had a more unexampled opportunity to observe history in the raw.

—Francis Henry Taylor, Director, Metropolitan Museum of Art, in forward to catalogue of a Metropolitan show of *Life*'s combat artists, 1943

September 1, 1939. The Blitzkreig. Hitler invades Poland, marking the beginning of World War II. That same day, Time Inc. circulation director Pierrepont Prentice wrote a memorandum to *Life* Managing Editor John Shaw Billings, urging him to consider the role of the artist in "America's Picture Magazine's" coverage of the war:

It is eighty years since the Civil War, but everybody still remembers the Civil War drawings in *Harper's* and *Leslie's Weekly*. It is five years since the World War, but everybody still remembers the war drawings in the illustrated London weeklies, and I sincerely hope that we are not so set in our devotion to the camera that we won't put a staff of first class illustrators to work right away drawing the war news.

Although *Life*'s signature feature as a magazine was its groundbreaking use of photography in journalism, the magazine's original prospectus stated the intention of "sending staff artists to make drawings of stories which cannot be satisfactorily photographed." Daniel Longwell, executive editor of the magazine at the time, went one step further, commissioning original works of museum quality by artists of great reputation for reproduction in the magazine. By early 1941, war loomed to such an extent that *Life* editors planned to devote the July 7 issue entirely to defense. With the cooperation of the Army Public Relations Office, some of America's brightest young artists were called in to paint our armed forces in action: Aaron Bohrod was hired to paint an Army town, Peter Hurd was assigned to Marine machine gun practice, and Henry Billings to the USS *North Carolina*, in the process of being built at the Brooklyn Navy Yard.

In the fall of that year, *Life* was eager to send correspondents to cover the lend-lease convoys, bringing supplies across the Atlantic in waters increasingly populated by Nazi submarines. Despite their refusal to grant the same permission to

Opposite: Davis, Detail of *After They've Gone*. Full image in The Artist's Eye

a *Life* photographer, Navy Public Relations permitted Tom Lea—a young artist from Texas—to cross aboard a destroyer. His paintings appeared in the May 25, 1942, issue.

When Pearl Harbor was bombed, *Life* wasted no time in sending artists out to paint America's early wartime activities. The artists who had been involved in the defense issue were all given assignments, and other artists were added to the staff. Among them was Edna Reidnel, who was commissioned to paint the war effort among workers in U.S. factories. Floyd Davis painted Naval bases in Bermuda. Tom Lea was again sent into danger—he was in the Pacific to witness the Battle of the Coral Sea. And in 1943 Millard Sheets was commissioned to go to India and China. These *Life* artists were given the status of war correspondents. They did not carry weapons, but they lived through the action—often drawing or painting only after they had stopped to help the soldiers they captured on canvas.

When the Army started its own war art program in 1943, three of *Life*'s artist correspondents—Aaron Bohrod, Edward Laning, and Millard Sheets—were incorporated into it. However, when Congress cut the funding for the Army program, many of the artists were stranded without assignment overseas. Daniel Longwell was traveling to Washington when he read the news, and he immediately went to see the assistant secretary of war, John J. McCloy, with an offer to employ all of the civilian artists (nineteen out of forty-two) in the program. Seventeen of them joined the staff of *Life* war artists. Among them were the well-known artists Henry Varnum Poor, Lucien Labaudt, and Reuben Kadish.

On June 19, 1943, a *Life* exhibit of war art opened at the National Gallery of Art in Washington, D.C. It went on to the Metropolitan Museum of Art in New York, and then to a national

Left: Smith, *Normandy Aid Station*

tour of major U.S. museums. *The New York Times* reviewer, after expressing his initial doubt that "the work of painters could hardly hope...to compete with the camera," wrote that his view had been "tellingly reshaped" by the *Life* show:

The exhibition as a whole is impressive. It contains much fine and serious work by American artists who have been provided with every opportunity to observe their material at close range, often intimately. It is the intimate, personal, penetratingly perceptive touch, indeed, that is equipped to furnish a chapter that would have been missing were the camera exclusively relied upon. This manifests itself preponderantly on the human side, as in the splendid series of small drawings by Tom Lea, and in water-colors by Paul Sample, several of which are superb, challenging even

Winslow Homer, of whose work in this medium they remind one at times.

The *Art Digest* enthused "...a thrilling story, and one more real than words, reproductions, news photographs, or dramatic radio scenarios can give. It is apparent to anyone looking upon the originals of these paintings...that they were painted under stress of emotion caused by the situation the artist was portraying."

Life trumpeted the news of the exhibitions in its October 9, 1943, edition, with a banner headline that read *"THE ART EXHIBIT THAT MILLIONS SAW!"* *Life*'s readers, the advertisement stated, "have been viewing, during the past two years, a remarkable exhibit of art, the results of a new venture in journalism.... Large as the attendance at these exhibits has been—26,733 New Yorkers visited the Metropolitan Museum of Art to see these paintings—it is a mere handful of people

Above: Sheets, *The Mourner*
Opposite: Sample, *Off Watch*

compared to the 22,000,000 civilians who had already seen these paintings in *Life*."

Throughout the war, *Life* continued to commission and reproduce works of art from combat artists, and in its collection are some of America's most enduring images from the war. Tom Lea's paintings from the invasion of Peleliu remain etched in the minds of many Americans of that era. *The Thousand Yard Stare* [p. 78], a portrait of a Marine suffering from shell shock, and *The Price* [p.38], a bloody painting showing a soldier at the moment of death, have become two of the most remembered images from World War II. The graphic realism of the pictures was controversial at the time. One reader wrote to the magazine, "God, how could you? Why such a picture?" But others were supportive, saying, "We can't have too much of stark reality. Keep it up."

The *Life* artists were not enlisted men, but they risked their lives on battlefields all around the world. Aaron Bohrod and Byron Thomas went to great lengths to be able to paint on Omaha Beach just two or three days after D-Day; Bernard Perlin lived and fought with guerillas in Greece; Floyd Davis flew in a bombing raid over Hamburg; Edward Laning was seriously wounded in Italy and was awarded a Purple Heart. One *Life* artist lost his life in the war. Lucien Labaudt, a beloved artist and muralist from San Francisco, was killed in a plane crash in India shortly after his arrival. Presumably the drawings he had completed went down with the plane.

Daniel Longwell's idea from the beginning had been to give the paintings to the government as a lasting record of the war—wartime magazines stated that it would be housed in "whatever memorial is erected to the heroes of World War II." Despite pressure to disperse the collection through gifts to individual museums, Longwell's vision was realized on December 7, 1960, when the collection—consisting of more than one thousand graphic paintings, water colors, and sketches—

was formally presented to the Department of Defense by Henry R. Luce, editor-in-chief of Time Inc., in a ceremony at the Pentagon. Today they are part of the U.S. Army Center for Military History archive in downtown Washington, D.C.

Above: Lea, *Fighter in the Sky, Solomon Island*

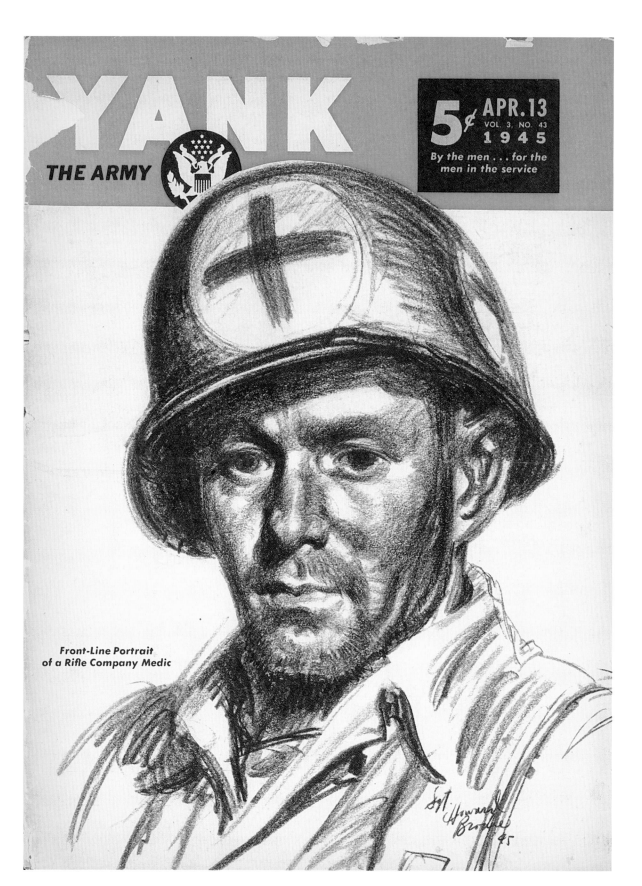

YANK

THE ARMY

5¢ · **APR. 13**
VOL. 3, NO. 43
1945

By the men . . . for the
men in the service

Front-Line Portrait
of a Rifle Company Medic

Yank Magazine: The Army Weekly

"By and for the enlisted man"

Yank magazine was founded in May 1942 by the War Department's Army Service Forces with a unique mission: to distribute an Army newspaper that would be read by enlisted men and that would be staffed, written, and edited completely by enlisted men. There would be no advertising; it would cost a nickel. The magazine was the brainchild of Egbert White, a New York advertising executive and *Stars and Stripes* staff member in WWI, who envisioned *Yank* as a fresher, more relevant version of that paper for this new World War.

Many in the armed forces were nervous at the thought of so much editorial control being placed in the hands of GIs, and before White was given the OK to proceed with the idea, he was required to present a preview issue to Secretary of War Henry L. Stimson for his approval.

A skeleton staff of civilians—among them executives from the advertising and publishing world, a songwriter, and a cartoonist—worked all night in the art department of *Mademoiselle* magazine to produce the first issue. Stimson signed off on the magazine with only one exception. According to Art Weithas, former art director of *Yank* and himself a combat artist, Mrs. Stimson felt that the full-page pin-ups of glamour girls included in the issue pandered to the "baser instincts" of the enlisted men. The Secretary of War ordered them deleted. In subsequent issues, amidst the chaos of wartime, the pin-up was revived. It became, along with George Baker's cartoon "Sad Sack," mail from the field, and news from home, one of the most beloved features of *Yank*.

In 1942, with photographic reproduction still in its infancy, artists and illustrators were a vital component of any magazine staff, and they were recruited along with writers and photographers to become official *Yank* correspondents. Some, like Howard Brodie—already very well known as a sports artist for the *San Francisco Chronicle*—were approached in their current jobs with the offer of enlisting and joining *Yank*'s New York staff. Others were drawn from boot camps and Army outposts.

In the summer of 1942 the *Yank* office at 205 E. 42nd street resembled a bustling, chaotic, unruly newspaper office. It did not at all resemble an Army organization. After multiple complaints within the War Department, a semblance of Army discipline was established, with regular Army drills in a playground off 42nd street, screenings of Army training films, and Army-style punishment

Opposite: Yank magazine cover, April 13, 1945

for latecomers and others not respecting Army rules and regulations: they were made to wash walls and scrub the men's bathroom.

As America's role in the global war grew, so did *Yank*. In November 1942 the first foreign edition of the magazine was printed in London. By war's end, the magazine was published in twenty-one editions, in every active theater of war and defense command around the world. It had a paid circulation of more than two million and was thought to be read by ten million. The ingenuity and determination necessary to establish presses and to distribute the magazine to all our soldiers, whether in Indian jungles or on Antarctic ice, was phenomenal. In more than one instance, *Yank* was printed on recently liberated presses, still warm from printing propaganda for the enemy. Ultimately, *Yank* employed 350 full staff members and more than 1,000 stringers.

Like all *Yank* staffers, the artist-correspondents rotated assignments. They would be sent overseas for a period of time and then return to the New York office. Often an artist was paired with a writer—Howard Brodie toured Guadalcanal with the writer Mack Morriss, and Barrett McGurn and Robert Greenhalgh worked together in the South Pacific—with the artist supplying the illustrations for the writer's story.

Throughout the war, *Yank* remained true to its original goal of creating a magazine produced exclusively by and for the enlisted man. Officers played only a background, supervisory role. Frank and often critical editorials on Army life, food, and pay made a regular appearance, and heated letters

Above: Greenhalgh, *Fire Direction Center, Bougainville*

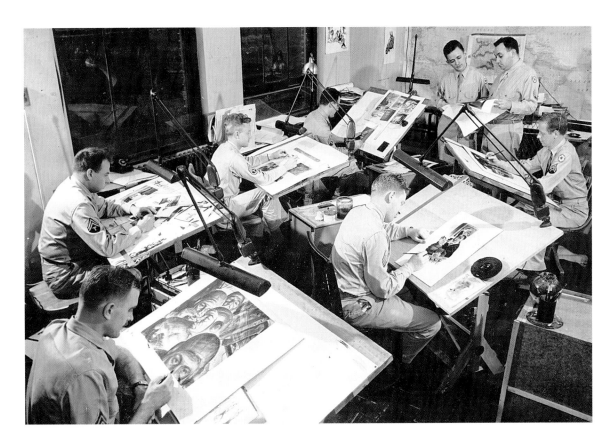

to the editor debated everything from racism in the army to the merits of particular pin-up girls.

Many soldiers sent their drawings in to *Yank* with the hope that they would be published, and in this way some of the members of the increasingly large magazine staff were discovered. Joe Stephanelli, today a noted American abstractionist in New York, was discovered after sending in his drawings of the Phillipines. As a *Yank* correspondent his life as a soldier was greatly improved. The magazine was so beloved by the infantrymen that the men who worked for it were treated like movie stars. They often had the freedom to go wherever they chose — and where they chose was frequently the front lines.

Four *Yank* correspondents were killed in action, including writer Pete Paris, on the Normandy beachead on D-Day in Europe, and Robert Krell, in an airborne assault across the Rhine. Many received Purple Hearts. The magazine they worked so hard and risked their lives to produce stands as a uniquely authentic record of World War II. Through their drawings, stories, and photographs we see the war, not as told by generals, historians, or Hollywood filmmakers, but as it smelled, tasted, and felt to the infantryman.

Above: Yank artists working in the studio
Below: Robert Greenhalgh and pals in uniform in New York

125

The artist has his duty to draw what he actually sees, and if he doesn't see it, he's not entitled to draw it. That's the way I feel.

Robert Greenhalgh

—Yank Magazine Artist

I was about twenty-six years old at the time. I wasn't married. I lived with my folks. There was a war going on, we knew that, because Great Britain had declared war upon Nazi Germany. But in the Midwest, there was still a feeling of isolation. I had the idea that it wasn't really fashionable to join the Army or the Navy. It didn't seem necessary because, after all, didn't Churchill say, "You give us the goods, and we'll finish the job"? We were the arsenal of democracy, weren't we?

I was drafted in the second draft, I missed the first. But, of course, not being married, I was soon drafted. And I was in the Army.

I had no special qualifications except just being young and able. I was sitting on my bunk on December 7, 1941. It was a Sunday morning and Sergeant Albers came in and said, "Hey, you guys! Did you hear what's happened?" And he said, "They bombed Pearl Harbor. We're in the war."

"Good-bye, dear, I'll be back in a year, for we're in the Army now." That was a popular song. "I'll Be Back in a Year." "Good-bye, dear, I'll be back in a year, for I'm in the Army now." Well, we knew we were going to be in the Army for a while.

I was out in the training field and all of a sudden a guy came up in a big command car, one of those Dodge command cars with the big antennas waving around, and Bucky, this sergeant, got out of the car and he said, "Hey, Corporal, get in. Secretary of War Stimson sent for you. We got this big order here saying you've got to go to New York City to be on *Yank* magazine."

Yank magazine was a news magazine that was published weekly by the enlisted men, not officers. Ordinary men. When you consider that most of our military is composed of the ordinary person, you realize that a lot of people didn't have a voice.

It was five cents. It had a pin-up. Pin-ups were something to look forward to. It had great photographs. It had drawings and writings by the enlisted man.

There's a pin-up there, Frances Rafferty. "Anybody know about Frances?" Everybody did in the Army when they got this picture. This was what they looked forward to. They didn't care who Frances was as long as Frances looked this way— it was all right.

Oh, that's exactly the kind of pin-up we all liked. She was perfect.

You were excited to be a part of it, because a lot of it had to do with reporting or drawing things that were happening. It was a little bit of a lark. After all, what could be better than being in the Army and drawing pictures. I felt sometimes apologetic, apologetic because other people had it tougher being in the war, in a war zone is a whole different ballgame than what we were doing. And nobody kidded themselves about that. And we were soon to find that out, when we were assigned to various places to report on the war.

They equipped me with all kinds of stuff. I had an M-1 [rifle] and hand grenades. And I carried my own sketch pad, that was all my ammunition, that was what we carried.

Oh, there's my old paintbox. I had this during the war and carried it around the Pacific. Old brushes, the old dog tags—36049195—don't have to read it, I know it—my old number. There it is, there— *Yank* magazine —carried that everywhere.

Guam—Notebook #3. A lot of memories in here. A lot of old water-soaked pages.

I would work at night by candlelight. That's about all you could work with. The main thing was to go back and find some kind of a quiet place where you could do something. And it was hard enough to get a place to work.

On Guam I had this experience of being with a young Marine Corps press photographer named Kelly. He and I went out together to the airfield on the Aroti Peninsula, where the Marines were, and there was an enormous amount of action out there. I went and made drawings, and when I came back I learned that this young fella [photographer] had been killed. I felt very badly about that.

An artist can sit back at his drawing board and draw any darn thing he thinks about, you know. Say, "Draw me a picture of the war," and you can sit back in your desk somewhere and draw a picture of a war or something. But the artist has his duty to draw what he actually sees, and if he doesn't see it, he's not entitled to draw it. That's the way I feel.

On one occasion, a plane came back in and

Above: Greenhalgh, drawing by candlelight

Above: On the Flight Deck
Below: Headquarters at Guam

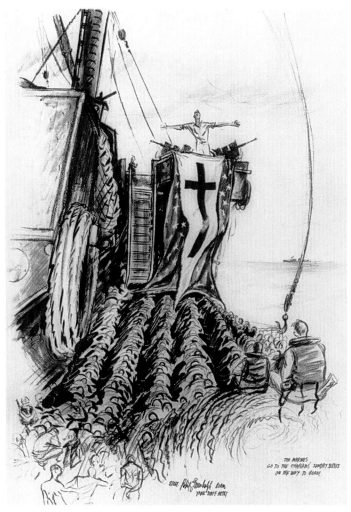

Some work was more finished in terms of being carried out to a higher polish. For instance, my work was very sketchy and loose. Howard Brodie was completely drawn and sketched out, which he did so beautifully. As I remember, Abbott Laboratories, at the time, was known for its many famous artists. Kerr Eby. Eby was, in my mind, one of the great, great military artists of any time.

And I remember seeing Kerr Eby and meeting him. I saw him on Guadalcanal in the press hut. I admired him very much.

His pictures were like etchings almost, or lithographs. He had marvelous expression in his hand. I don't know how he did it. I felt almost like an incompetent nincompoop compared to him.

He also was a pretty brave and daring kind of guy.

plunged into some planes on the carrier deck, exploded, and threw gasoline all over the place. And I remember eight or more men running, burning, on fire like torches. And I can remember this one poor fellow was on fire and he was lying down on the deck and the photographer came along and was taking his picture, and the guy, who was dying, waved him away, said, "Don't"—and his face was all white, like burnt up. And he was mortally hurt. I didn't draw that. I didn't want to draw that. I don't know why, I guess it's because I didn't feel like...I guess it's a different thing. I don't think that that kind of intimate gore is too good.

I'm here to tell you there's no such thing as a painting or drawing that's done on the spot. In the South Pacific, in the second battle of Bougainville, I was so nervous. I was kind of hunkering down to get away from whatever it was, and worried, and nervous and jumpy and the tank going this way and that way.

And I can remember I heard about people doing things on the spot and I tried to make this drawing and I just couldn't do it. And I've got a drawing in my notebook that shows you that. Here's a scribble here, right here. There it is, that's as good as I can do—that's in ink. Says, "proof you can't do it on the spot."

And so then here's another. This is called,

Above: Sunday Service

"more proof that you can't do it on the spot." That's as good as I could do. Can you make that out? I don't know what it is myself. The only person I ever saw do anything on the spot was a guy, a Marine. He was on top of this telephone pole, he was sketching this picture. He's sitting around on top of this telephone pole in the middle of this pitched battle and he's the only guy I ever saw do anything like that.

When you get up into an area where there is a great deal of action, on the front lines, I was quite surprised, the attitudes of people change. In other words, there's a certain amount of kindness and softness and consideration for one another.

It seems like heaven, almost. That's funny, isn't it, heaven? Why is that "heaven"? That isn't heaven, it's hell.

But people are nice, good. In fact you forget about who the other person is. That person might not be your same color or background. But you forget about that. You just forget about it. Everybody seems to be okay. And then you leave that area and you come back into the rear and it becomes very apparent that what you've seen is something that's quite unique and special.

Maybe they feel as though this may be their last moment on earth.

I've seen enough of it. I don't want to see any more of it, I'll tell you that. It's something you don't even want to mention much.

Well, the worst thing is that you wonder why so many good, good people are gone. Why—why—why was it necessary for all these people to disappear. All your friends.

I was in the Army for about almost four and a half years. And I felt pretty lost by the time I was discharged. I was almost afraid to get out of the Army. It seemed to me that that was life. I'd had most of my life. I couldn't remember much else.

I look back on it and all I can think about is how lucky I have been, that's all. I can remember my dad said, "What'd you do, Bob [in the Army]?" I said, "Well, I don't know, Dad. I was an artist and they had me going out and making pictures. I don't think that I was doing anything like the other fellas were doing. I was not an infantry soldier. Those guys know what it's about." But then my dad said to me, he said, "Well, Bob, you took your chances." I said, "Well, I guess that's how you can say it, I took my chances."

When I was in school, I always had the idea that I would like to be a war artist. If I could just do something like that, that would be great, being a war artist. Wouldn't that be good? But of course, at that time, I had no idea that such a thing might ever come to pass. I didn't deliberately train to do such a thing. It was a good dream.

I feel we are all artists, and I feel if we love what we're doing, we don't even think in

terms of the danger. That's secondary.

Howard Brodie

— U.S. Army

I wanted to be an artist since the second grade, in grammar school in Marin County, across the bay from San Francisco.

I was a sports artist for the *San Francisco Chronicle*. I drew Joe Lewis, Joe DiMaggio, I traveled with the Yankees...you name them, I was drawing them all. I received a phone call from the editor of *Yank* magazine, which was the Army weekly, and he said that he really wanted me to join the Army, and he would get me onto *Yank*. So I joined the Army, and that's what brought me into the war.

I love the military. In World War II, on *Yank* magazine, we were called special forces, and we could have been the misfits of life, or the elite of life, whatever the hell we were. We were artists, writers, Broadway playwrights. General Eisenhower decreed that no one could be an officer on *Yank* magazine; if you got to be an officer, out you went from *Yank*. So we were all enlisted men. They felt the enlisted man would not be properly represented unless he was represented by another enlisted man. By the end of the war, it was an extremely successful magazine.

When I first arrived [Guadalcanal] and moved up to the front and I heard firing, I was frozen with fear. And I mean really frozen with fear. I listened to it, I didn't want to advance, I didn't advance, I couldn't advance. I just was frozen with fear.

I was on assault with an infantry company and there were many casualties on this assault. There was 88 fire from the enemy, there was small arms fire, numbers of men went down. I would say that between one-fourth and one-third of our men were casualties. We finally got to a barn. German 88 fire came through one wall on one side, and then our own tanks came up on the other and they didn't know we were in there and they were firing at us, so we had friend and foe firing at us. And it was too much for some soldiers to stand.

I remember the young soldier well, he screamed, he was just out of control and he screamed and so forth, and there was another soldier next to him who consoled him and embraced him [p. 134]. That was a moving moment for me, to see that compassion in combat. And these are the things that a person feels when he's in proximity to death, his buddy, that next human being, that person in the foxhole is the most important person in your life.

I didn't really have a big sketch pad. I would just make little notes.

Impressions were burned into my brain. I recall a GI floating in the black smoke of an exploding mine. He just rose and floated in it. A piece of flesh sliced by a sergeant behind him. The sergeant later told me that the man just disappeared in front of him. That was so etched in my mind that I was able to draw that picture later.

I can recall vividly seeing a lookout, a GI, in the barn peering through a crack, and he turned back

to his squad leader and said, "There's a Gerry out there," which was a nickname for a German, "taking down his suspenders. I think he's going to take a crap." And he ordered mortars on this poor German soldier. It took a brand of courage [for the German soldier] to do this simple, natural act. That's why I drew that [p. 136].

I heard a fine friend of mine who was a war artist talk fairly recently; he was saying, "No one ever draws on the spot." I would take issue with him and say that one can draw on the spot, because I have drawn some of my best things on the spot, while it happened.

My most searing memory of any war was during the Battle of the Bulge when Germans posing as GIs infiltrated our lines. I heard we were going to execute three of them and I sped up to the MP post and saw these three men brought

Above: Moving Up
Opposite, top: Howard Brodie
Opposite, bottom: Compassion

by a squad to three posts. And they were lashed to the posts and the firing squad came up.

A defenseless human is entirely different than a man in action. To see these three young men calculatedly reduced to quivering corpses before my eyes really burned into my being. That's the only drawing I've had that's been censored. All coverage of the execution was censored.

A particular GI moved me deeply when he breathed to me, "You know, I can never kill a man. I aim over their heads and hope they surrender." And for a man to say that in the heat of combat, that moved me profoundly. Not that a soldier should think that, but I wonder if most humans haven't felt that, or thought that. I'm sure he wasn't alone. Because in the heat of it,

that's what he breathed to me, when his life was in danger. I'll never forget. In fact afterwards, I asked him if I could say that. And he said, "Yes, you can."

These fellas awarded me the Bronze Star, yes. But I tell you, I received the Bronze Star humbly because they wrote a report on me for the Bronze Star that was so…you'd think I was Florence Nightingale with all the healing I did over there.

I've sketched actually four wars. World War II in the Pacific and in Europe, and I've sketched the Korean War, I was with the French in In-dochina, I was with our troops in Vietnam. And subsequently General Sullivan commissioned me to sketch the contemporary soldier. So I've spent several weeks with troops in the Mojave Desert of California. It seems that the military is the-matic in my life. I feel the human is more beau-tiful in proximity to life and death. His emotions are more deeply felt. I've seen men who would take from you behind the lines give to you on the line. I've seen men give profoundly.

Ah, war, for all its negation, there is a beauty there when we're facing life and death that I've seen and experienced and am thankful for.

Above, left: Squad Leader
Above, right: Execution
Opposite, top: Wounded Man
Opposite, bottom: Nature Call

Compassion

The eye of the hurricane is calm. In the middle of the battlefield horror, World War II artists found kindness, compassion, and soldiers caring for one another. The best of the human spirit shone through the darkest of human events.

Some artists were assigned exclusively to front-line medicine by Abbott Laboratories of Illinois, but inevitably every artist was drawn to the struggle to preserve human life.

The images that hold the eye the longest are neither glamorous nor glorifying. They are heart-wrenching depictions of the price paid in human lives and suffering, sobering studies of soldiers engaged in the art of war.

Opposite: Benney, Detail of *Battle Cave*

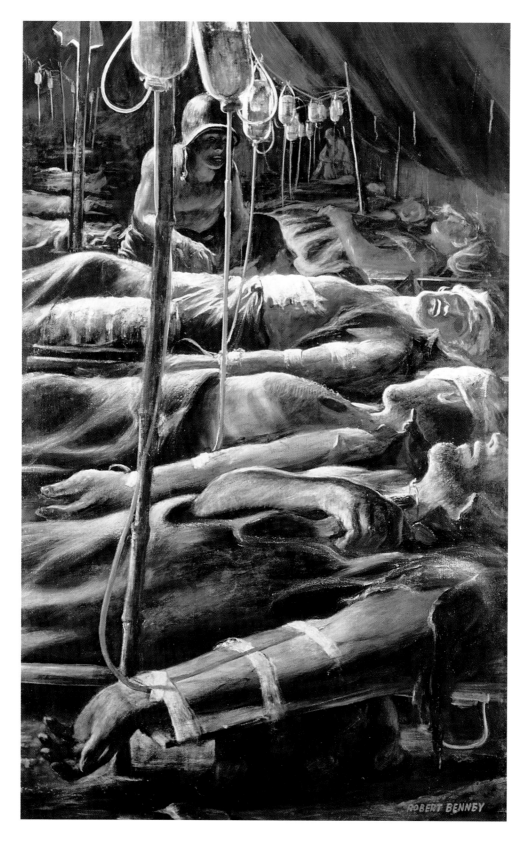

Above: Benney, *Shock Tent*

Above: Benney, *Battle Cave*
Below: Hirsch, *Field Examination*

Above: Eby, *Jeep Turned Ambulance*
Opposite, top: Hirsch, *Company in the Parlor*
Opposite, bottom: L.B. Smith, *Return Cargo*

Above: Boggs, *Jungle—Ally of the Enemy*

Above: Boggs, *Race Against Death*

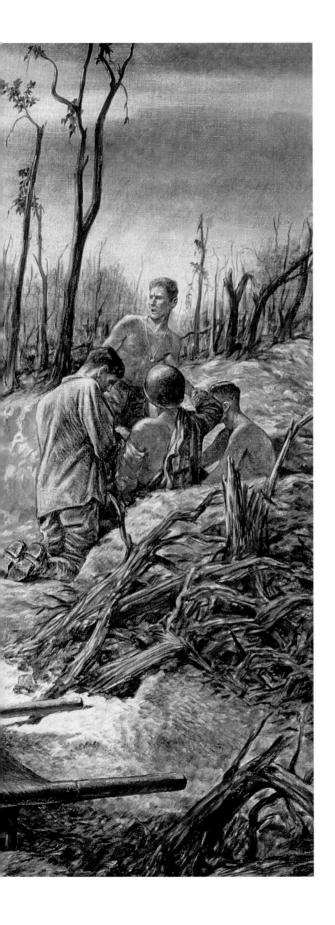

Above: Laning, *Botanical Garden*
Below: Eby, *Helping Wounded Man*
Left: Lea, *Sundown on Peleiu*

Above: Hirsch, *After the Fascist*
Below: Brodie, *American Tank Man*
Opposite: Sample, *Soldier with Child*

Abbott Laboratories War Art Program

It was not an easy task these artists were called upon to undertake. Seven of them spent many long days in hospital trains and ships and in the drug laboratories. Five of them braved the dangers of submarine-infested seas to reach combat areas. They were subjected to the same hardships and dangers as the front line units to which they were attached. Armed with only palette and brush they lived in New Guinea foxholes and Normandy cellars. They took everything the enemy had to offer and risked their lives voluntarily and repeatedly to complete their mission.

—Surgeon General N.T. Kirk, introduction to Abbott Laboratories-sponsored catalogue of medical paintings

Legend has it that on December 7, 1941, Thomas Hart Benton, America's outspoken renegade artist, was on a lecture platform giving a speech when news of the Japanese attack on Pearl Harbor was announced. He was so shaken by the news that he stopped speaking, left the platform, canceled all future lecture dates, and sequestered himself in his Kansas City studio, where he worked without stopping for nine weeks. When he emerged, he had painted a powerful and violent series of seven paintings on war, which he called *The Year of Peril*.

Benton's agents realized the power of the paintings as a propaganda tool, and reproductions of them began appearing in U.S. newspapers. Charles S. Downs, art patron and the director of advertising at Abbott Laboratories, saw a newspaper clipping and immediately called Benton, suggesting that Abbott buy all seven paintings for a series of War Bond posters.

Abbott, a large pharmaceutical company headquartered in North Chicago, Illinois, was inti-mately involved in the war effort. In addition to shipping drugs and pharmaceutical supplies to the medical corps overseas, Abbott focused much of its research efforts towards solutions that would benefit the men fighting overseas — testing compounds for malaria drugs, for example.

Abbott also had a long corporate history of supporting American artists, commissioning them to create works of art without commercial restriction. Under Downs' direction, the company published an attractive, glossy magazine called *What's New*, which was distributed free to pharmacists and physicians across the country. Alongside articles on new Abbott products and research, the company published full-color reproductions of the art it had commissioned in co-operation with the Associated American Artists gallery in New York, who represented the artists.

Downs shared Benton's belief that good artwork could be a powerful tool in bolstering public support for the war effort and in encouraging the public to buy war bonds. In the April 1942

issue of *What's New, The Year of Peril* paintings appeared sandwiched between an article on "Cod Liver Oil Ointment and Paper Tissue Dressing for Burns" and another on hay fever plants and pollen called "Enemy Aliens and Native Saboteurs." Physicians and patients leafing through the magazine must have been shocked by the paintings and by the equally intense text Benton wrote to accompany them:

I have made these pictures, as I have at other times spoken, in the interest of realistic seeing and with the hope that I might be of help in pulling some Americans out of their shells of pretense and make believe. There are no bathing beauties dressed up in soldier outfits in these pictures. There are no silk-stockinged legs. There are no pretty boys out of collar advertisements to suggest that this war is a gigolo party. There is no

hiding of the fact that war is killing and the grim will to kill . . . I have made these pictures for all Americans who will look at them. They are dedicated, however, to those new Americans who, born again through appreciation of their country's great need, find themselves with new shares of patriotism and intelligence, and new wills to see what is what and to come to grips with it, in this Year of Peril.

Encouraged by the overwhelmingly positive national response to these paintings, Abbott went on to become a major force in the commissioning and distribution of combat art. Downs initiated a formal agreement with the Federal Government by which Abbott would sponsor the creation of an art collection that would serve as a "comprehensive record of war activities, both at home and on the battlefield." The contract made it clear that the artwork was

Above: Robert Benney sketching

Opposite: Drawings by Kerr Eby

to be for the benefit of the American public, not Abbott Laboratories, and that the work would belong to the people:

The entire collection of paintings, drawings, and other works created by leading American artists is to become the property of the United States Government.

All costs and expenses of the various projects will be paid by Abbott Laboratories, including, without limitation, payment to artists for their compensation, framing of pictures, transportation and subsistence expenses, cost of uniforms and art supplies, and insurance of artists.

Neither Abbott Laboratories nor the individual artists shall make any use or dis-

tribution of the pictures for the purpose of deriving a profit therefrom.

Abbott Laboratories agrees not to advertise the making of the gift of the pictures to the United States Government. The company shall, however, have a non-exclusive right to distribute reproductions of approved pictures to the press, and the Government shall have the right to make reproductions and effect distribution in any way it may choose.

The Government reserves the right to discontinue any or all projects at any time [at] its discretion.

The endeavor was actually a collaboration between three entities: Abbott paid the artists for

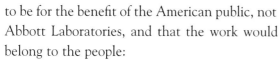

Above, left: Joseph Hirsch
Above, right: Kerr Eby
Opposite: Naval Aviation Display, drugstore

their time and expenses; Associated American Artists (AAA) secured the artists and helped to administer the project; and the War Department provided transportation and hosted the artists overseas.

Throughout the war, this unique infrastructure worked very well. On the home front, many of the war bond posters we remember today—"Remember Me? I was at Bataan" and "Till we Meet Again"—were produced by means of this contract. More remarkably, more than two dozen artists sponsored by Abbott Laboratories went into battle as combat artists with the Army, Navy, and Marines. Among them were Robert Benney, Kerr Eby, Franklin Boggs, Reginald Marsh, Georges Schreiber, Joseph Hirsch, and John Steuart Curry. Under the direction of Reeves Lowenthal at Associated American

Artists, they were assigned to focus on particular themes such as "Army Medicine" or "Navy Aviation." (Thomas Hart Benton and several other artists were assigned to paint the work of Navy submariners.) The resulting collections of paintings were hung as individual shows in public art galleries and museums around the country.

Abbott artwork focusing on the work of the medical corps provoked an overwhelmingly positive response from the press and public. One critic called them "striking, vibrant, I might say beautiful paintings of the healing hand of medicine amid the ugliness of war," and noted:

An Army colonel not long back from the Burma Theatre was standing in front of Howard Baer's painting of an army ambulance bogged down on a Burma jungle trail during the monsoon. "That's it, all right," he exclaimed, "I can see it—smell it—taste it!"

As part of the effort to use the paintings to increase the sale of war bonds, Abbott had hundreds of 8-by-10 color reproductions of the paintings printed and distributed them in folios to a wide variety of venues, including drugstores, car dealerships, millineries, and department stores around the country, with instructions for turning them into window displays. In this way, the art reached Americans at a grass-roots level with news of what war was like for their boys overseas, often in color more realistic and vibrant than the newspapers and newsreels of the day, as this letter, written to Abbott in January 1945, attests:

Dear Sirs:

I deem it a privilege and an honor to be able to display the Navy's Pacific Theatre Sixth War Loan Show.

The coloring is very beautiful and the figures most realistic and awe-inspiring. The display vividly portrayed to the civilian population what our boys are going through, and what a sacred obligation we have to back them up with the purchase of bonds.

By actual observation, this window created a great deal of interest, and certainly was food for serious thought, and I feel sure it stimulated the sale of bonds.

I close with the words of the "Immortal Lincoln"

"Let us have faith that right makes might; and in that faith let us to the end, dare to do our duty as we understand it."
Sincerely yours,
S.P. Tomaso
Tomaso's Pharmacy

The Abbott artists were not monitored or censored to any real degree, and therefore the work they created was highly individualistic and eclectic. Many of the AAA artists were from the school of New Realism popular in the American art scene between 1930 and 1945; others were more expressionistic.

Today it seems incredible to see photographs of graphic and often disturbing paintings hanging in display windows between advertisements for soda pop and skin cream. But the combat artists felt driven to communicate the truth of war to the American people, and the public, likewise, felt compelled to understand it. Kerr Eby, whose drawing of a dead Marine trapped on a metal tetrahedra [hedgehog] at Tarawa remains one of the strongest images from the war, said when interviewed, "What difference does the medium make? It is the truth. I made these for the Marines. To hell with art."

After the war, the Abbott collections were donated, as promised, to the War Department, dispersed to the Army and Navy collections according to the branch of service depicted by each piece. Numbering well over one hundred paintings, they are an extraordinary and powerful account of World War II.

Opposite: Naval Aviation Display, Coldblatt, Chicago

I was always challenging myself. Is this the best I can do? Is this good enough?

Franklin Boggs

—Abbott Laboratories

I can't remember when I didn't draw. I grew up on a farm down in Indiana, and my folks always supplied me with crayons and drawing paper and always were encouraging me, which is very fortunate. I always had in mind I was gonna go to art school, and I did.

Reeves Lowenthal called me on the phone. He says, "Get ready. We're gonna make a war correspondent out of you."

I was very pleased because my draft board was out there, and they were sending me letters all the time stating that I was going to be called up for the draft. So they had to send an Army officer from New York down to my draft board to persuade them that I was going to be a war correspondent and they couldn't have me.

It was really Reeves Lowenthal's imagination. He went to Abbott Laboratories and convinced them that they could make a real contribution by doing something about the Medical Corps in the war. Abbott thought it was a great idea and went ahead with it.

The assignment was to cover the Medical Corps in the Southwest Pacific. And that meant the whole package, from the time that someone was wounded and a battalion aide went out to bring him in to get his first attention until he got on a hospital ship and was sent back home.

When I really got to where the action was taking place, I flew in a B-25 bomber with General Chase and three of his colonels. On the plane they said, "Here's your parachute and your kit. If you go

down in the jungle, you've got everything you need to catch fish and what have you." And they said, "By the way, here's an automatic weapon, and here's some hand grenades. You may need those."

When we arrived, we flew in a hundred feet from the ground, and I could look right down into the faces of the Japanese as we went by.

When we stepped off the plane I had a shock, it was one of odor. The jungle had all been blasted away and the hot sun shining down on all that foliage brought back great memories to me as a boy on a farm when I was only about ten years old. We had a terrible hail storm one night, and it cut down all the maple trees and all the corn, and the same smell of that hot tropical sun on all that green foliage was Hoosier memories.

I met a colonel and I told him I wanted to see everything on the front line. And he said, "I have a group of people up on top of a mountain that have been cut off, and you and I are going up to see what's going on up there." So we started up this mountain, through this dense growth of bamboo, and at one time there was a terrible cry in the jungle, and everybody said, "Hit the dirt." And I thought, "Oh, my God, this is gonna be it," you know?

Well, after we were there a while, one of the natives got the word to the Australians that it was only a jungle bird.

But in the meantime, while I'm lying down in this steaming hot jungle, I'm looking at this guy's foot

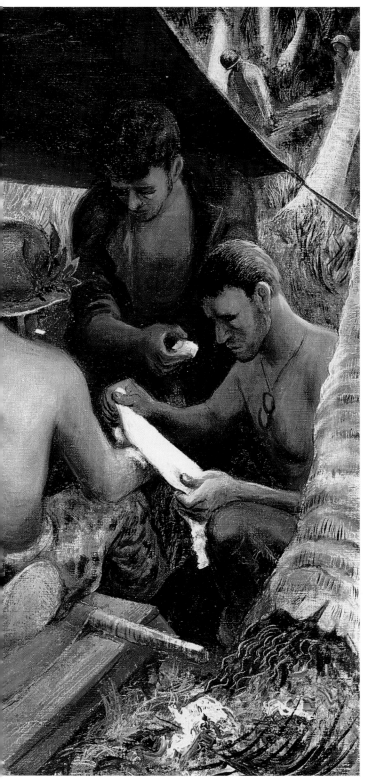

[Papua New Guinea native] right in front of my eyes, who had never had a shoe on all his life, of course, and it had red clay on it, in the cracks, and I thought, "Boy, those are rather interesting cracks," you know. I got so interested in those cracks, thank heavens, I forgot my fears for a moment.

That evening, after we went back down, colonel says, "Here comes a load of dead." And there was what looked like a big farm truck with siding on it, and it was passing by, and my eyes weren't more than this far [eighteen inches] away from the slats, and I'm looking through, and I had a terrible emotional shock of seeing a high school ring on a hand, right there. And it upsets me to think about it to this day.

We had the rank of captain, all war correspondents. There were some guys I talked to who thought I was crazy. "What are you doing out

Above: Franklin Boggs
Left: Battalion Aid Station

here when you don't have to be?" I said, "Well, I've come out to show what has happened to the Medical Corps and all the suffering." Then they thought, "That's pretty good, that's OK."

One of the things that I depicted was pill call. Malaria was so prevalent out there, and the Japanese had cut off all our supply for quinine from the Philippines, so we invented something called Adabrin. When you take these pills it doesn't cure malaria, it just keeps the fever and the shock down so it's bearable.

So everybody is supposed to take these little yellow pills, but a lot of guys thought, "If I can hang on to this malaria and can have it really

bad, they won't send me to the front." Well, the Army wanted them to get well and go back to the front, even if they were yellow-green in color. So they had to have pill call, and they had to watch these guys put it in their mouth and with a canteen of water swallow those pills.

One particular night when I arrived back from the front, I asked the doctor, "Where can I sleep?" He said, "Why don't we just put you into the ward with the patients?" I said, "That's all right with me. I'm exhausted." So they put me in the ward where everybody's sleeping under mosquito netting. During the night the nurses would

Above: Pill Call
Opposite: Night Duty

come in periodically and I'd be looking through these nettings and see them taking care of the patients. I did a painting of that.

I carried in my pockets little notebooks, and I had a very good camera. I took a lot of pictures and I made notes, such things as when a bandage is on, and it starts bleeding through the bandage, what kind of shapes do those make? And you couldn't possibly make up beforehand what kind of shapes they'd make. They're really very unique sometimes. And what happens when a person is in shock, and his hair's all matted with perspiration and the way it mats on his head.

These are the kind of notes I took down, but my finished paintings were not of a scene, my fin-ished paintings were a combination of all sorts of things relating to that particular event.

Color, edges, shapes, texture — all those things have so many variables, endless variables. You pick out the ones that fit the particular painting or particular idea. You make sketches. Thinking about how much area is going to be color, important color, how much area is going to be controlled by shapes, things like that.

Emotion is part of expression. An artist is supposed to express something. If he does it successfully, it has aesthetic properties.

I was always challenging myself. Is this the best I can do? Is this good enough?

One evening I remember walking along the beach where the invasion had been. There was an

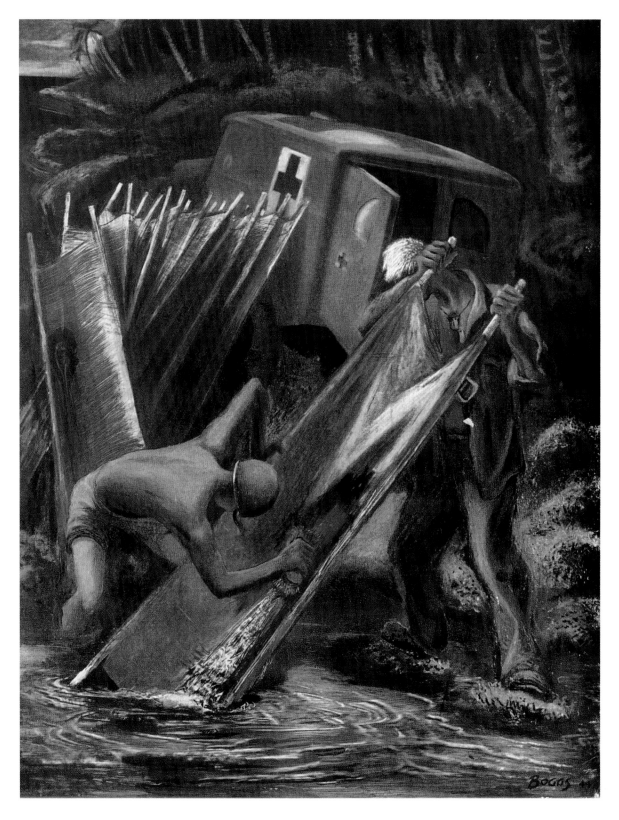

Above: End of a Busy Day
Opposite: Return to the Golden Gate

ambulance backing up to the surf where two corpsmen are out washing the blood out of the litters for that day. One of the guys I had standing in the water, he was naked. And they said, "We can't have any nakedness in this series of paintings," and I thought, "That's weird. You can kill people, but you can't show one naked person." But anyway, I put drawers on him to satisfy them, and it really upset me. But the painting has drawers.

On the ship, there were many patients who were in bed all the time and they had to have a lot of attention from nurses and so forth. So they said, "Now, when we get within the Golden Gate Bridge, please tell us," and so some of them convinced the other people to carry them up on deck. It was so dramatic when we got near San Francisco and they really could see the Golden Gate. That was home. That was a symbol of, "My God, I've made it back alive."

I lived outside of Knoxville, Tennessee, up on a little mountain outside of town, and I could look down and see the road coming out from town, and I would think, "This would be a good place to have a gun mounted to stop the traffic." I mean, I got to thinking military terms, you know? It was—it was crazy, really crazy. The war paintings I did got acclaim in art magazines and so forth. I don't mean that I was one of the great American artists. But I was known, period.

It changed my life. It gave me a position to come and teach at Beloit College. For thirty-two years I was at Beloit College. I was an artist in residence, and I could have commissions off site, which I was

constantly doing, murals and other things. So I had a very busy life. I'm very lucky.

I don't think we think of ourselves as being so damned unique. I've been trained to do art. It's all I've done all my life. I ought to be fairly decent at it.

This *Private Ryan* thing is great anti-war. The first thirty minutes is just fantastic in that it's good for the populace to see the horror of war because there's so much glamour involved with war. Whether it's Napoleon or Ulysses S. Grant, they glamorize the war. Think of the thousands and thousands of suffering souls that died.

I would say that the very fact that I was with the Medical Corps I think was anti-war. My paintings—I like to think of them being for peace. I didn't want to glamorize war in any way.

Away from Battle

When there was not war — when the battle was like the memory of a dream — they settled into an uneasy weariness, reacquainted themselves with the loneliness and despair, and attended to a soldier's plainer tasks. They shaved and showered, scrubbed up their fatigues, wrote letters, and lost their pay in poker games. The sweetest time of all was furlough — girls, civilian food, and cold beer.

That time between, when war pauses to gather its breath, yielded some of World War II's most poignant images.

Opposite: Bohrod, Detail of *Idle Hour Park*

Above: Martin, *Redhead Picking Flowers*
Opposite, top: Bohrod, *Idle Hour Park*
Opposite, bottom: Draper, *Boxing Match*

Above: Davis, *Paris*

Right: Davis, "Bob Hope Entertains the Troops"

Above: Davis, *GI in Perfume Store*

Above: Sample, *Off Watch*
Below: Hurd, *Took Force Encampment*

Above: Lea, *The Ready Room*
Below: Davis, *United Service Club*
Right: Murray, *A Lighter Moment During Arduous Training*

Above: Simon, USS Missouri
Opposite, top: Sample, *Canton Island*
Opposite, bottom: Sample, *Divine Services*

Artist Biographies

Franklin Boggs

Franklin Boggs received his art education at the Ft. Wayne Art School and at the Pennsylvania Academy of Fine Arts. He was awarded two European Traveling Fellowships and was in Europe at the outbreak of the war in 1939. His earliest work was recording the activities of the Tennessee Valley Authority and doing murals for the U.S. Post Office. He became a war artist-correspondent for Abbott Laboratories early in 1944 and documented the work of the Army Medical Department in the South Pacific. After the war Boggs was commissioned to paint in South America and became a full professor and artist in residence at Beloit College, where he continued his work as a muralist. His works have been exhibited in many leading U.S. museums including the Metropolitan, Corcoran, Legion of Honor, and Chicago Art Institute. His murals are in eight U.S. states; two are in Finland.

Howard Brodie

When World War II started, Howard Brodie was a sports artist for the *San Francisco Chronicle*. He became one of *Yank* magazine's best-known artists during the war. He painted everything from Guadalcanal to the Battle of the Bulge and had an uncanny ability to capture the emotions of his subjects and record a scene with great attention to detail. He put himself in combat situations many times and received the Bronze Star for his coverage of World War II. After the war, Brodie became a courtroom artist and recorded many famous trials, including those of the Chicago 7, Charles Manson, and General Westmoreland. Brodie never fully severed his ties to the military and was a combat artist in Korea, French Indochina, and Vietnam. Brodie continues to work today. Recently he was commissioned by General Sullivan to draw the modern soldier in combat training at Fort Irwin in the Mojave Desert.

Manuel Bromberg

Manuel Bromberg was born on March 6, 1917, in Centerville, Iowa. After studying at the Cleveland School of Art and the Colorado Springs Fine Arts Center, he painted murals for the WPA. He entered the Army in April 1942 and was appointed to the War Artist Unit a year later. He painted, sketched, and drew the war throughout the European theater and was part of the invasion of Normandy at Omaha Beach. He was awarded the Legion of Merit for creating an extraordinarily fine graphic record of the war and his work was published in many magazines and newspapers, including *Life* magazine and *The New York Times*. After being discharged from the Army as a Master Sergeant in 1945, Bromberg won a Guggenheim Fellowship in creative painting and became a professor at North Carolina State University's School of Design. Still an active artist, he now works with fiberglass and creates large sculptural castings of rock and cliff formations.

William Draper

Draper attended Harvard and studied art at the National Academy of Design and in Europe. He went into the Navy at the start of World War II and saw and painted combat in both the Aleutians and the South Pacific. Draper became a highly acclaimed portrait artist in America after the war. His portrait of Kennedy hangs in the White House; his study of Nixon is in the National Gallery. Now in his eighties, he continues to paint in his New York studio.

Richard Gibney

Gibney grew up in Saratoga Springs, New York, and graduated from Syracuse University before being drafted into the Marines at the start of the war. Originally trained as a demolitions engineer and later part of the Marine Art program, Gibney saw and painted combat in many battles in the South Pacific. He took part in five D-Day landings, including Tarawa and Saipan, and was a survivor of the "Westlock Tragedy" in which the ship he was on was heavily damaged in an explosion. He returned to the U.S. after the war, and continued his art studies at the Pennsylvania Academy of Art and then in Europe as part of a travel scholarship. He applied his experiences studying stained glass and fresco murals in Europe to the stained glass windows he designed for the Marine training camp at Parris Island's chapel and in over twenty public murals in the United States. In 1993 he completed what he calls "The Odyssey," a semi-autobiographical series of fifty-two paintings that detail the saga of a young marine in World War II.

Robert Greenhalgh

Robert Greenhalgh, a graduate of the University of Missouri School of Journalism, was beginning his career as an illustrator selling drawings to the *Chicago Tribune* and *Esquire* magazine when he was drafted into the Army. As a well regarded *Yank* staff artist during the war, Greenhalgh painted and fought in Guam and Bougainville and received the Award of Distinctive Merit from the Art Directors Club for his work depicting the war. After being discharged from the Army, Greenhalgh had a successful career as a TV art director at the Young and Rubicam advertising agency. Now retired, he lives in New City, New York.

Edward Reep

Soon after graduating from the Art Center School, and five months before the attack on Pearl Harbor, Reep enlisted in the Army as a private. After getting an assignment as an overseas artist, Reep sketched and painted throughout North Africa and Italy. He often found himself in the thick of battle and was repeatedly strafed, bombed, and shot at while painting the war. He was awarded the Bronze Star, was promoted twice on the battlefield, and left the Army as a captain. Reep returned home to work on a Guggenheim Fellowship, awarded to him on the basis of the paintings he executed in Italy. After the war he had a career teaching painting and drawing at the Art Center College, East Carolina University, and the California Institute of the Arts. He lives in Bakersfield, California.

Acknowledgements

They Drew Fire owes its life and inspiration to my good friend John Frook. This forgotten piece of history was uncovered by John, and through his vision and guidance; this project came to life. I will always be indebted to John, and his wife Norma, for all their help.

This project would not have come to pass without the generous funding provided by Abbott Laboratories. We are grateful for their commitment and shared belief that this is an important piece of American History that needed to be told. Our sincere thank you to Karmin Maritato, Mimi Welty, and Catherine Babington of Abbott Laboratories for all their support and assistance.

In researching the Combat Artists of WWII, we were helped by many people around the country. Mary Lou Gjernes, curator at the Army Center for Military History in Washington D.C, helped us to navigate the Army's huge collection. We are likewise indebted to Jack Dyer, curator of the US Marine Corps Museum, and Gale Munro, curator of the Navy Art Collection. We began to understand the history of combat artists and found several of the artists featured in this book through Peter Harrington, of the Anne K. Brown War Art Collection at Brown University. Our thanks to Bill Hooper, of the Time/Life Archive for his help researching the LIFE war art collection. Instrumental to our understanding of *Yank* magazine were Janet and Art Weithas; Art's book, *Close to Glory*, is the definitive history of Yank told by the men who lived it.

Our indebtedness and thank you extend across the country to many people, especially Bonni Cohen, Victor Livingston, Jon Else, Michael Chin, Todd Wagner, Jason Robards, Jamie Stobie, Marco and Terri d'Ambrosio, Brian Jim, Debbie Pfeifer, Tom Stritickus, Deborah Pardes, Jan Petrucelli, Mary Powell, Adam Messinger, Marilyn Meitz, Lisa Jones, Jonathan Halperin, Tony Kaplan, Judy Karp, Doug Dunderdale, Jon Haptas, Mike Boyle, Jon and Abe Shenk, Jill Tufts, Hilary Morgan, John Chater, Dave Davis, Sheila Rittenberg, Selena Lauterer, Maya Angelou, Bob and Jan Gilka, Buck Tharp, Allen and MaryAnn Dutton, Kathy Kifer, Don Latarski, Drs. Peter and Pamela Cary, Ray and Chris Scofield, McDonald Frame Shop, Photoregon, David Friend, Todd Brewster, Orland R. Bulkeley, Rich Clarkson, Tony Sheets, Peter Franck, Mr. And Mrs. Bud Lanker, Rev. Merril Lanker, Nancy Bryan, Linda Umble, Norman and Barbara Savage, Maj. Barry Johnson, Wendy J. Brodie, Jane Bromberg, Sondra Boggs, Isabel Brodie, Diana Gibney, Catherine Greenhalgh, Karen Patricia Reep, Robert Bennney, Brockie Stevenson, Joe Stephanelli, Bernard Perlin, Edward Brodney, Anne Poor, Alex Russo, Tom Lea, Harry Jackson, Tom and Mona Miksch, and the artists who shared their lives, artwork and stories with us —Ed Reep, Richard Gibney, Robert Greenhalgh, William Draper, Manuel Bromberg, Franklin Boggs and Howard Brodie. A very special thank you to Lynne Lamb and Marc Hedlund for all their hours of work and assistance. And those family members who not only physically worked on this project, but whose spirit lifted us all throughout this project: Lynda and Dustin Lanker; Julie and Jacki Coburn; and Blaine, Joanna, Lisa, and D. Jay Newnham.